DANIELLE WIGZELL

Keeping It Real: The Honest Guide to Frugal Family Living

First published by Danielle Wigzell 2026

The information contained in this book is based on the author's personal experience and is intended for general informational purposes only. It does not constitute financial, legal or professional advice. Readers are encouraged to seek independent professional advice before making any financial decisions. The author accepts no liability for any loss or damage caused by reliance on the information contained in this book.

First edition

ISBN: 978-0-473-79438-5

This book was professionally typeset on Reedsy.
Find out more at reedsy.com

For my husband, and for our children — for being adaptable beyond your years, for the sacrifices you've made without always understanding why, and for finding joy in a life that has never looked quite like everyone else's. You are my greatest achievement, and my very best reason to keep going.

Contents

1 Keeping It Real: My Story 1
2 Keeping Everyone Fed 6
3 Keeping the Lights On 48
4 Keeping a Roof Over Your Head 57
5 Keeping You Moving 66
6 Keeping Up Appearances 73
7 Keeping the Kids Happy and Entertained 79
8 Keeping the Kids Educated 85
9 Keeping the Family Healthy 90
10 Keeping Afloat 94
11 Keeping Yourself Sane 101
12 Keeping Going 105

1

Keeping It Real: My Story

If you'd told me twenty years ago that I'd one day be writing a book about frugal living, I'd probably have laughed. Not because I didn't need the advice — but because I was young, in a good paying job and hadn't really ever thought about having children, let alone being broke and trying to feed that family.

My story begins in the UK where I grew up. What I class to be an ordinary upbringing, nothing particularly remarkable about my childhood or my relationship with money. I was raised in a conventional family - two parents, two kids. My parents owned a house, in conjunction with the bank, they both worked, food and clothing and everything else I required was provided.

So when my struggles with money began, it was kind of out of the blue. Life happened. And it happened fast.

I'd completed university, I was about six years into my career in marketing, I was in a healthy, long term relationship and we had a house, a mortgage, each owned a car and had enough disposable income to enjoy life. Then the rug was pulled. Redundancy and an unexpected pregnancy arrived in the same breath. No job, a baby, and the kind of financial panic that hits you at 3am when you're already exhausted and feeling sick. Can we survive on one income?

We made it work, we had to. It wasn't always pretty, and it certainly wasn't always comfortable, but we learned fast that necessity is a brilliant teacher. We were managing. We were paying the bills, our baby's immediate needs were provided for and there was still enough left over for the occasional Sunday lunch at the pub.

Life carried on. Somewhere in the middle of nappies and tight budgets, we got engaged. My parents had saved for my wedding day — a generous and thoughtful gift — but we were determined to make every penny count. A lavish UK wedding didn't feel right for us. So instead, we took the budget, booked flights to New Zealand, got married there with just close family, and spent six weeks road-tripping the country. A destination wedding and a honeymoon adventure for a fraction of what the same money would have bought us at home. It was the first time I realised that thinking differently about money didn't mean missing out — sometimes it meant getting more.

Back in the UK, 18 month old in tow, the struggle continued. Britain in 2011 was hardly welcoming — the financial crash had left its mark, belts were tightening everywhere, and the sense that hard work would eventually get you ahead felt increasingly hollow. We were treading water, we knew it but we couldn't see a way out.

Then my husband was offered a job in New Zealand.

We looked at each other, looked at our life, and made a decision that was equal parts terrifying and exciting. A new country. A better job. A genuine fresh start. Why not?

We gave ourselves a safety net, we told ourselves it was just for a year. A try-before-you-buy approach to emigration — if it didn't work out, we'd just come home. No harm done.

We started packing, I began to feel sick and then discovered we were expecting baby number two. No time to think about that right then, we were on the move, we'd work it out on the other side.

New Zealand was everything we'd hoped for in theory. In practice, three years into our new life, Wellington was not quite the lifestyle we'd imagined. I'd gone back into the workforce but my salary barely covered childcare for two and the commute, leaving little for the life we'd actually come here for. We decided New Zealand was home but that the true New Zealand we'd come for was actually on South Island. We sold our UK house, and used the equity to buy a place of our own in North Otago. We wanted the lifestyle dream, the ultimate work/life balance and we committed to the re-start.

Within weeks my husband was made redundant and my hours were slashed.

I worked two jobs to keep us afloat, running on caffeine and stubbornness, determined we wouldn't lose everything we'd worked for. My husband went back to Wellington for another job - to temporarily ease the financial pressure - but the reality was that we were no better off, now juggling our own mortgage and a rental. We were back to treading water but this time we were sinking, heads dipping in and out of the water month in and month out..

Auckland called next, promising opportunity and a higher salary. What it delivered was expensive rent, traffic, and the creeping feeling that we were working harder and harder just to stay in a place we weren't enjoying. The rat race had followed us to the other side of the world and we weren't any better off.

So we did something that most people thought was either

brave or completely mad. We bought bare land in Hokitika, on the wild West Coast, my husband quit a well paid job and we built a life from scratch. Literally. We constructed a garage, made it home, and lived off grid for three years. No mains power, no utility bills. No mortgage payments eating us alive. Just us, our kids, and a determination to do things differently.

We were running a photography business by this time. It was thriving. We were finally living the life we'd been chasing for years — self employed, low outgoings, time with our kids, and for the first time in a long time, a little disposable income to actually enjoy in a beautiful part of the world.

Then Covid hit. The photography industry stopped overnight. No events, no portraits — no income. Like so many small business owners we watched everything we'd worked for quietly collapse, and there was nothing we could do about it.

Covid had taken our business but it hadn't taken our spirit. We still had the land, the garage, the off grid life we'd built. We were regrouping, we were planning out our next chapter...

Then came the accident. A bad one. Suddenly I was living off ACC payments, unable to work, trying to hold everything together — and discovering, somewhat against the odds, that I was pregnant with baby number three.

Surprise doesn't quite cover it.

We loved our Hokitika life but we had to be honest with ourselves. No bathroom, no laundry, wild weather and an untamed landscape — it was a lot at the best of times. For someone facing a very limited income, a long road to physical recovery, or a newborn, it was just about manageable. To experience all those at the same time, it simply wasn't. We moved, had a baby, and added 'survived all of that' to our list of achievements

All of this happened over the space of a decade — comfort and financial ease, then struggle and anxiety, then back to comfort again, then back to struggle. What all of this taught me — through the redundancies, the emigrations, the off grid years, the business failure, the injury, the unexpected baby — is that financial resilience isn't about having lots of money. It's about knowing what to do when you don't. It's about feeding your family well on almost nothing. Keeping the lights on when the budget says you can't. Finding joy in a life that looks nothing like the glossy version you planned.

This book is everything I learned the hard way, so you don't have to.

It's practical, it's honest, and it's written by someone who has genuinely been there — not someone who chose minimalism as a lifestyle trend, but someone who had frugality handed to them by circumstances and learned to make it work.

Whether you're facing redundancy, a growing family on a tight budget, or just the creeping sense that your money disappears before you understand where it went — this book is for you.

So let's start where every family's budget starts and ends — keeping everyone fed

2

Keeping Everyone Fed

Food is non-negotiable. Whatever else is happening with the budget, whatever else has to wait or go without, your family needs to eat — and eat well. This chapter is about making that happen without hemorrhaging money at the supermarket every week. It's not an exhaustive list of every money saving trick ever written, and I'm not going to pretend I do all of this all of the time. But these are the habits, strategies and shortcuts that have genuinely worked for our family, through some very tight times indeed. Take what's useful, leave what isn't.

Knowing Your Grocery Budget

Before you set foot in a supermarket, before you plan a single meal, you need to know your number. How much do you actually have to spend on food each week? Not a rough guess, not a hopeful estimate — an actual figure based on what's left after your bills are paid.

If you don't know that number, start there. Look at your bank account, add up your fixed outgoings — rent or mortgage, utilities, insurance, fuel — and see what's left. That's your living money, and a portion of that is your food budget.

There's no universal right answer for what that number should be. It depends on where you live, how many people you're feeding, and the ages of your kids. A family of three with a toddler spends very differently to a family of five with teenagers who eat like it's their full time job.

What matters is that you have a number and you stick to it. Everything else in this chapter works backwards from that figure. Meal planning, shopping across multiple supermarkets, buying in bulk — all of it only works if you know what you're working with.

Write it down. Put it in your phone. Whatever works for you — just know your number before you do anything else.

Our grocery budget has varied enormously over the years depending on our circumstances. Back in 2014 in North Otago, I was feeding two adults, two young children and a dog on $80 a week. By 2026, with those same kids now teenagers and two more little ones added to the mix, that budget had grown to $200 a week. On paper that looks like progress — more than double the budget. In reality it's anything but. Inflation has pushed the cost of basics up significantly, and feeding teenagers is a different proposition entirely to feeding young children. More mouths, bigger appetites, higher prices — the $200 we spend today buys considerably less, feeds considerably more, and feels considerably tighter than that $80 ever did. The number changed. The squeeze didn't.

Meal Planning

Meal planning is the single most effective thing you can do to take control of your food budget. It sounds obvious, but knowing what you're going to eat before you shop means you only buy what you need — and that alone can transform how far your grocery budget stretches.

The first step is deciding how often you shop. Weekly shopping suits most families — you plan seven meals, buy what you need, and you're done. If you prefer a monthly big shop, you can still meal plan week by week, working from what you bought at the start of the month. Either works, as long as the plan comes before the shop.

Personally, we get paid fortnightly but I choose to shop weekly. I simply split the fortnightly budget in half — half one week, half the next. Fruit and vegetables generally last a week so I don't factor in top up shops. It keeps things simple and means I always know exactly what I have to spend.

Before you plan a single meal, open your fridge, freezer and pantry. Check what you already have. Check expiry dates and pull anything that needs using up to the front. There is no point planning a bolognese and buying mince if you've already got mince in the freezer that's been there for three weeks — use that first. Building your meal plan around what you already have before you spend another cent is one of the easiest ways to reduce waste and save money at the same time.

Next, check the specials at your supermarket. Most supermarkets publish their weekly deals online before the week begins. If chicken is half price this week, chicken features in your meal plan this week. Let the specials guide you where you can rather than rigidly sticking to meals regardless of cost. On a Monday it's now my ritual to quickly check the specials mailer from Woolworths, I draw inspiration from what's genuinely a good deal.

Then look at your week. What have you actually got going on? A sports night, a late finish at work, a school event — these all affect what's realistic on any given evening. A slow cooker meal on a busy day, something quick on a late night, something more involved on a weekend when you have time. Plan around your actual life, not an imaginary one. Some meals are naturally seasonal too — a hearty lamb stew belongs in winter, a fresh pasta salad in summer. Planning around the seasons means you're more likely to be cooking with produce that's at its cheapest and best.

Get the family involved if you can. Ask everyone for their favourite meals and their not-so-favourites — nobody wants to cook something nobody will eat. That said, be realistic about budget. Their favourites might not always be possible every week, and that's okay. Work in the popular meals when the budget allows and save the more expensive requests for when things are a little more flexible.

Finally, decide how much variety you actually want. Some families are perfectly happy eating the same rotation of meals every week — it's simple, everyone knows what to expect, and the shopping practically does itself. Others want more choice and variety. Both approaches are completely valid. The point of meal planning isn't to make food boring, it's to make it manageable. Find the rhythm that works for your family and stick to it.

I've tried a few different approaches to meal planning over the years. A set weekly rotation sounds great in theory — simple, predictable, easy to shop for — but I found it too repetitive and honestly a bit soul destroying after a while. I like variety. So instead of a fixed rotation I plan loosely, grouping meals so that a more expensive dinner is balanced out by a couple of cheaper ones either side. A roast on Sunday might be followed by a pasta dish and a soup later in the week to balance the budget back out. It's not rigid but it works for us.

Writing a Shopping List

A shopping list is non-negotiable. Shopping without one is the single fastest way to overspend — you wander, you browse, you remember things you don't need and forget things you do. A list keeps you focused, keeps you fast, and keeps you on budget.

Write your list based on your meal plan. If you've planned your meals first, your list practically writes itself — you know exactly what you need and you buy exactly that.

Without a list you are at the mercy of the supermarket, and supermarkets are very good at parting you from your money. The promotional ends of aisles are designed to catch your eye — bright colours, bold saving claims, tempting new products. Suddenly you're thinking "oh I'd like to try that" or "if I buy the Watties brand I'll be saving 50 cents" — on an item you have absolutely no need for this week. That's not a saving. That's just spending money you hadn't planned to spend. A list, and a little discipline, keeps you walking past all of that with purpose.

Don't shop hungry either. It sounds like a cliché because it's true. Everything looks appealing when you're hungry and your trolley will reflect that at the checkout.

We keep a magnetic shopping list on the fridge. When something runs out, it goes straight on the list. Simple. When it comes to the weekly shop I work through the list alongside my meal plan and make a judgment call on each item — is it needed this week or can it roll over? Some things are always required regardless of the meal plan, butter and flour for baking being a good example. Others are meal specific — pesto only makes the list on a week I have pesto pasta planned. It stops me restocking things I don't immediately need and keeps the shop lean.

Shopping Across Multiple Supermarkets

Not all supermarkets are created equal, and loyalty to one store can cost you more than you realise. Different supermarkets have different strengths — one might consistently be cheaper for pantry staples, another might have better fresh produce, another might run better specials on meat. Once you know your local options it's worth splitting your shop accordingly. However when doing this you do need to determine if the additional costs to travel between stores or the additional time to your schedule are worth the savings by moving stores.

Before you set foot in any store, do your homework. Most supermarkets publish their weekly deals in mailers, online, and through their apps. Spend five minutes at the start of the week checking what's on special where. Apps like the Grocery app — which compares prices across multiple supermarkets — can do a lot of that legwork for you on your regular weekly items, though other similar tools are available and worth exploring to find what works best in your area. Knowing where the best deals are before you shop means you're making intentional decisions rather than just grabbing whatever is in front of you.

Surprisingly our local dairy, which is known for being a little more expensive due to its rural location, has cocoa powder priced a few dollars below my usual grocery store so that's an item that is always purchased there, despite pretty much every other item being higher in price.

When shopping across multiple supermarkets, there are a couple of tactics that work really well for me.

1. **Shopping Online**

If your supermarket offers online shopping, it's worth considering even if it comes with a small service fee. Shopping online removes almost every temptation the supermarket throws at you — no promotional aisle ends, no bright packaging catching your eye, no "oh I'll just grab that while I'm here" moments. You search for what you need, you add it to your cart, you review your cart, check the total price and you check out. That's it. For many families the service fee is easily offset by the impulse purchases they simply don't make when they're not physically in the store.

Personally if I'm shopping in store I'm a sucker for the reduced to clear items in the supermarket and often pick those up as 'extras' as they are often luxury items that don't fit within our typically weekly budget but are heavily discounted - things like Lewis Road Creamery cream. It blows out the budget and can derail all my hard work. There is a time and a place (and a saving) to be made from the reduced to clear category but I'll come to that later.

1. **The Conveyor Belt Method**

If you do shop in store, the conveyor belt at checkout can actually work in your favour if you use it strategically. When you get to the checkout, load your most essential items onto the belt first —

the things you absolutely cannot leave without. Keep an eye on the running total as items are scanned and if you're approaching your budget, ask the operator to pause. Ideally if you've stuck to your list there shouldn't be anything left in your trolley at that point — but prices aren't always what you expect and you might find yourself a few dollars over.

Whatever is left in your trolley or on the conveyor belt after your budget has been met is by definition the least essential part of your shop. You can choose to put those items through or leave them at the checkout. Yes, the staff would prefer you didn't — but it is absolutely okay to do it. There is no shame in it. It keeps you on budget, and more importantly it makes you genuinely aware of what you're buying, what things cost and what can be culled when money is tight. If something gets left behind every single week, that's a signal it probably doesn't need to be in your trolley in the first place.

Reduced to Clear

If you shop in store, the reduced to clear section deserves a significant place in your grocery strategy. These are often the best savings in the entire supermarket and with a little flexibility they can genuinely transform your weekly shop.

Different stores handle their reduced stock differently. Some have specific times they discount items whilst others do it throughout the day. Some group everything together — chilled items in one area, dry goods in another, discounted fresh produce somewhere else. Others simply mark items down in place on the shelf, leaving you to spot the yellow or orange reduced stickers as you work your way around the store. It really depends on your supermarket, so it's worth getting to know how yours operates.

If your store groups reduced items together, make this your first stop. Before you do anything else, head straight there and scan what's available. Start by looking for items that are already on your shopping list — if the cream you were going to buy anyway is sitting in the reduced section, that's a straightforward win. Then look a little wider. If there's a more premium brand of something you need at a reduced price, check whether it's actually cheaper than what you had planned to buy. If the reduced price matches or beats your usual buy, grab it. If it's still more expensive than your planned item, leave it alone — a discount on something you weren't going to buy is still spending money you hadn't planned to spend.

Sometimes the reduced section will prompt you to rethink a meal or two entirely. If you spot heavily reduced ham, salami or bacon for example, a homemade pizza night suddenly makes a lot of sense — swap it in, remove a more expensive planned meal, and you've just made your budget stretch a little further without any real effort.

When items are discounted in place on the shelf rather than grouped together, it's a different proposition. Pivoting your meal plan mid shop means backtracking, putting items back, rethinking on the fly — it takes time and energy that isn't always available, especially if you're shopping with kids in tow. In that situation I tend to only pick up a reduced in situ item if it's something I was already planning to buy. The effort of re planning on the spot usually isn't worth it unless the saving is significant.

Remember that the reduced to clear items are often just on or past their use by or best before dates - this means that if you're buying these items, you'll need to use them pretty early in the week. In most instances it's easy to switch your meal plan around to accommodate the products that will expire first.

Own Brand vs Named Brands

One of the easiest ways to reduce your grocery bill is to swap named brands for own brand alternatives. In most cases the product is virtually identical — often made in the same factory — and the only real difference is the packaging and the price. Pasta, rice, flour, sugar, tinned tomatoes, frozen vegetables, cleaning products — own brand versions of these are almost always a safe swap and the savings across a full weekly shop add up quickly.

But let's be honest. Not every own brand swap is a winner, and pretending otherwise isn't helpful. There are some products where the quality difference is real, where the named brand genuinely tastes better or performs better, and where the extra cost is worth it to you. The key is being intentional about which battles you pick rather than blindly buying named brands out of habit.

For me, baked beans is a swap I'm not willing to make. Budget baked beans are not baked beans — they are a disappointing, often near neon orange, sugary liquid with beans floating in it. I will wait until Heinz, specifically the English recipe, is on sale and I will buy those instead. That is a deliberate, considered choice. The rest of the time I'm reaching for the own brand without a second thought.

Toothpaste is another one. I almost always buy Colgate. I know it's not meaningfully different from own brand toothpaste. I buy it anyway, largely because it's what I grew up with. Which brings me to something I find genuinely fascinating.

My university dissertation was on consumer buying behaviour, and one of the most consistent findings in that field is how significantly our shopping habits are shaped by what our parents bought. The brands on the shelves of your childhood home become your default, your comfort, your benchmark for what something should taste or look like. You're not choosing Colgate because you've conducted a rigorous comparison — you're choosing it because your mum chose it, you brushed your teeth with it daily for years.. You can absolutely break that cycle, and often you should, but you have to spot it first. Next time you reach for a named brand on autopilot, pause for a second and ask yourself — am I buying this because it's genuinely better, or because it's just familiar?

Go through your regular shop and identify your non-negotiable named brands — the ones where the quality difference is real and worth the extra cost to you. Buy those. Everything else, try the own brand. You might be surprised how few things you actually notice the difference on.

Buying in Bulk

Buying in bulk is one of the most reliable ways to reduce your cost per meal, but it requires a little more thought than simply grabbing the biggest packet on the shelf and assuming it's the best value....because sometimes it isn't.

The most important habit to develop is checking the price per gram or price per 100g rather than the headline price. Most supermarkets display this on the shelf label and it's the only fair way to compare products of different sizes. A larger pack is usually cheaper per gram — but not always. Occasionally when a smaller size is on special you'll find that buying two of the smaller packets actually works out cheaper than the standard larger one. You'll only know this if you're in the habit of checking the unit price rather than just the sticker price. It takes a few extra seconds but it can make a real difference over time. The price per 100g is often also listed online so you can do the same comparison when online shopping as well as in-store.

When it comes to bulk buying, dried goods deserve a special mention. Dried chickpeas, kidney beans, black beans and lentils are some of the most frugal items in the entire supermarket and they are considerably cheaper than their tinned counterparts. Yes, they require soaking and a little forward planning — but the cost difference is significant and the quantities you get are generous. These are your meal padders, your frugal protein wins, the ingredients that turn a small amount of meat into a meal that feeds the whole family. A bag of dried lentils costs a fraction of the equivalent in tins and will go considerably further. If you're not already cooking with dried pulses regularly, it's one of the most impactful changes you can make to your grocery budget.

Cooking From Scratch

Cooking from scratch is one of the cornerstones of frugal living. Pre-made meals, packet sauces, ready-made pastry, store bought cakes and slices — the convenience premium on all of these is significant. When you make things yourself from basic ingredients you are almost always paying a fraction of the price, and the quality is usually better too.

From scratch cooking can cover a huge range — bread, pastry, pasta, sauces, cakes, scones, slices, scrolls and more. The more you make yourself, the less you're paying for someone else's labour and packaging. It does require time and a willingness to be in the kitchen, but once these things become habit rather than effort the time investment feels much less significant.

A word of honesty here though — not everything is worth making from scratch, and only you can decide where your time versus money trade off sits. I've made pasta from scratch. It's lovely. It's also time consuming and fiddly and given the amount of time I already spend in the kitchen it's not something I choose to add to my repertoire. Shop bought pasta it is, and I have absolutely no guilt about that. Pick your from scratch battles wisely.

The one thing that has probably saved us loads over the last few years is homemade bread. Yes, we now have a bread-maker but before the bread maker, I made it by hand. In fact, I was trying to save for a bread maker for a while before I was actually gifted one. We've had the same Panasonic bread-maker for about ten years now and it makes a loaf every single day. If you don't already own one it's worth keeping an eye out for one secondhand — they come up regularly and are rarely worn out.

One thing worth noting if you do use a bread maker — look closely at your recipes. Our machine came with a recipe book and the standard white bread recipe has considerably more ingredients than the Italian bread version. The Italian bread is our everyday loaf purely because it costs less to make and the difference in taste and texture is minimal. Simple as that. That said, I do switch to the white bread recipe when I'm making dinner rolls — it produces a lighter, fluffier result that's worth the extra ingredients on those occasions.

There are genuine health benefits to cooking from scratch too — real ingredients, no hidden additives, sugars or chemicals you can't pronounce. But this book is about frugality not nutrition, so I'll leave you to do your own research on that one.

Eating Seasonally

Eating seasonally is one of those habits that sounds a little worthy but is actually just good common sense from a budget perspective. When produce is in season locally it is at its cheapest, its most abundant, and frankly its most delicious. When it's out of season it's been shipped from somewhere else, stored for longer, and you are paying a premium for the privilege.

The difference in price can be significant. Tomatoes in the height of summer are cheap and plentiful. Tomatoes in the middle of winter are expensive, flavourless and not worth your money. The same goes for stone fruits, berries, corn, zucchini/courgettes, and a host of other produce that has a clear seasonal peak. Buy them when they're in season, enjoy them at their best, and build your meal plan around what's cheap and abundant rather than forcing a recipe that calls for out-of-season ingredients.

It also naturally adds variety to your cooking across the year. Winter meals lean towards root vegetables, hearty soups and stews served with brassicas. Summer cooking shifts towards salads, fresh herbs, stone fruits and lighter meals. Your meal plan follows the seasons almost instinctively once you get into the habit of shopping this way and it can really shake up the monotony of the same foods in your meal plan rotation.

Getting to know the seasonal calendar for your area is worth a small amount of effort upfront. A quick search for what's in season where you live, by month, will give you a rough guide to work from. Over time you won't need to look it up — you'll just know.

Some meals in our house are firmly seasonal. A slow cooked beef stew padded out with delicious dumpling firmly belongs in winter. A fresh tomato pasta sauce belongs in summer when tomatoes are so cheap and ripe they practically make themselves. Letting the seasons guide your cooking rather than fighting against them makes the whole process feel more natural — and your grocery bill will reflect it.

Grow Your Own

Growing your own produce is the natural extension of eating seasonally, and for some things it's absolutely worth doing. For others, honestly, it isn't — and it's important to be realistic about that rather than romanticising the idea of a vegetable garden without considering the actual time, effort and cost involved.

The maths don't always stack up in your favour. Onions are a good example — I can buy odd bunch onions (you know the ones that are slightly smaller than the 'norm' or slightly less round) from the supermarket for a fraction of what it would cost me in time, space and effort to grow my own. For something like that, buying is simply the smarter choice.

But some things genuinely are worth growing. Potatoes are an excellent example — one sprouting potato planted in the ground can produce a significant crop, and if you've already got some going soft and sprouting in the back of your cupboard you may as well put them to use rather than throw them away. The return on investment is hard to beat.

Zucchini/courgettes are another one I grow without hesitation. They are virtually indestructible, require almost no attention, and in the right climate they go absolutely gangbusters — you'll have more than you know what to do with at the height of summer. Which, conveniently, is exactly when you want to be building meals around them.

The key with grow your own is to be selective. Work out what grows well in your area with minimal effort, cross reference that with what you actually eat regularly, and focus your energy there. A few well chosen, low maintenance crops will serve your budget far better than an ambitious vegetable garden that becomes a second job.

Preserving and Making the Most of Abundance

When seasonal produce is abundant — whether from your own garden, a neighbour's tree, or simply a glut at the supermarket — preserving it is one of the most satisfying and economical things you can do. The work you put in during a season of plenty pays dividends for months afterwards.

We are lucky enough to live in an area where apple trees grow at the side of the road. Every autumn I harvest them and make the most of every single part of the fruit. The apples get dehydrated into apple crisps for snacking, cooked down into pie fillings that go straight into the freezer for winter desserts, grated into oat slices, and baked into cakes. The skins and cores don't get wasted either — boiled up they produce a beautiful apple drink that costs nothing but a little time. Nothing gets thrown away.

That approach — using every part, preserving what you can't use immediately, and building it into your cooking over the coming weeks and months — is frugal living at its most satisfying. It connects you to the seasons, reduces waste, and puts food on the table that costs you almost nothing.

Preserving doesn't have to be complicated. Freezing is the simplest starting point — most cooked fruit fillings, soups, sauces and baked goods freeze beautifully. Dehydrating is another low effort option if you have a dehydrator or even just an oven on a low heat. Jams and chutneys require a little more effort but last for months and make excellent gifts too.

Keep your eyes open for abundance around you — a neighbour with a lemon tree who can't use them all, a glut of tomatoes at the local food pantry, a roadside fruit tree that nobody else is picking. These things are there if you look for them.

Cheap Pantry Staples

A well stocked pantry is one of the most powerful tools in your frugal kitchen. When your cupboards have a solid base of staples you can build a meal from almost nothing, stretch ingredients further, and avoid those expensive last minute trips to the supermarket for one missing item. We all know how that goes. You need one thing. You pop in for one thing. You come out with eleven things and a slightly guilty expression at the checkout. A stocked pantry means those trips happen far less often.

There are a few different methods for doing this but I've found that the 'overstock' method works best for me and my cooking style.

The Overstock Method

The overstock method is a really simple system that works best for our family. For every key pantry item — particularly baking supplies like flour, sugar, yeast, baking powder and so on — I keep two at any one time. One open and in use in the working pantry, and one sitting in reserve in the overstocks cupboard.

The rule is simple. When you finish the open item and reach for the reserve, that's the moment it goes on the shopping list for the next grocery cycle. Not when you're completely out — when you've just opened your last one. That way you always have something to work with and you're never caught short mid bake or mid recipe.

If money is tight in the next shopping cycle, the fact that you've literally just opened a fresh item means you can make the call to hold off restocking for a week if you simply can't afford to add that item to your shopping cart. That flexibility is the whole point. But — and this is important — make absolutely sure you roll it over to the following shop. The overstock method only works if you actually restock before you run out entirely. Let it slip and you're back to the emergency supermarket dash, which we are trying to avoid at all costs.

Everyone in our family is aware of the overstock method, I'm not the only one who steps foot in the kitchen, I'm not the only baker or chef so it's vitally important that the rest of my family follows the overstock rules....they understand how annoyed I get if I use the brown sugar up, reach for my overstock and the cupboard is bare. As we currently live rurally just 'popping to the shop' isn't even an option. It's important to note that this doesn't just apply to your edible food stocks, it applies to all your day to day items too - toilet paper, washing up liquid, deodorant.

Staples Worth Always Having In

Beyond the overstock principle, there are certain ingredients that earn their place in any frugal pantry simply because of how far they stretch and how many meals they can anchor. These will vary from family to family depending on what you cook, but as a starting point consider keeping:

- Flour, sugar, baking powder, yeast and butter for baking
- Dried pasta, rice and noodles as meal bases
- Tinned tomatoes and coconut milk as sauce foundations
- Dried lentils, chickpeas, black beans and kidney beans for bulk and protein
- Oats for porridge, baking and padding
- Olive oil, soy sauce, vinegar and basic spices for flavour
- Honey, peanut butter and jam as store cupboard staples

These are the ingredients that sit quietly in your pantry and show up in meal after meal. Keep them stocked and you always have somewhere to start.

Making Meals Stretch Further

One of the most effective frugal cooking skills you can develop is knowing how to make a meal go further without anyone at the table feeling short changed. The secret is padding and bulking — adding cheaper, nutritious ingredients to extend a more expensive base without losing the flavour or satisfaction of the original dish.

Done well, nobody notices. Done really well, the meal is actually better for it.

Getting the Most From One Chicken

One of our most reliable weekly buys is a 2.3kg frozen chicken. It gets roasted, and then the real work begins — every scrap of meat is stripped from the carcass and turned into multiple meals across the week. People are often genuinely surprised when I tell them I can feed our entire family a hearty, satisfying meal using just one chicken breast. Not a chicken breast each. One breast, between the whole family.

The key is that the chicken is never the meal — it's an ingredient in the meal. Shredded into a pasta sauce, stirred through a fried rice, folded into a pie filling — a small amount of chicken goes a very long way when it's paired with the right supporting ingredients. The carcass itself doesn't get wasted either. Boiled up with some vegetables and aromatics it makes a stock that forms the base of soups, risottos and sauces throughout the week. One chicken, bought cheaply from frozen, can realistically anchor four or five meals if you're intentional about it.

Mince Based Dishes

Spaghetti bolognese and cottage pie are two of the most budget friendly meals in any family repertoire, and they can be stretched even further with a little clever bulking. Adding dried or cooked lentils to your mince is the easiest starting point — they absorb the flavours of the sauce beautifully and are virtually undetectable to even the fussiest eater. Porridge oats are another surprisingly effective option, particularly in cottage pie — they bulk the mince out, add texture, and cost almost nothing. Start with a small amount until you find the ratio that works for your family.

Chili

Chili is one of the most forgiving meals to bulk out because beans are already an expected ingredient. Black beans, kidney beans, cannellini beans, borlotti beans — pretty much any bean works here. Use a smaller amount of mince than the recipe calls for and make up the difference with whatever beans you have in the pantry, tinned or dried. A generous amount of tinned tomatoes helps too. A pot of chili that was meant to serve four can easily stretch to six with very little effort.

Curry

A chicken curry is a perfect example of a meal that can be padded out without losing any of its appeal. Chickpeas are the natural addition — they absorb the sauce, add protein, and complement the spices beautifully. Diced potato is another excellent option, particularly in a mild curry, and it's one of the cheapest ingredients you can add to any dish. Frozen peas, spinach and cauliflower all work well too depending on the style of curry. The rule of thumb is to use less meat than the recipe suggests and replace the volume with vegetables or legumes.

Soups and Stews

Soups and stews are perhaps the easiest meals to stretch of all. A handful of red lentils added to almost any soup will thicken it, bulk it out and add protein without changing the flavour significantly. Leftover vegetables, the last of a bag of frozen peas, a tin of beans — all of these can go in. Pearl barley is another brilliant addition to stews — it swells considerably during cooking and turns a modest pot into a genuinely filling meal.

Baking and Breakfast

Stretching food isn't limited to dinner. Grating courgette, apple or carrot into muffins and cakes adds moisture and bulk while using up produce that might otherwise go to waste. Adding an extra banana to a banana bread recipe, mixing oats into burger patties or meatballs, stirring chia seeds into porridge — small additions that make a little go a lot further.

The broader principle is this — identify the most expensive ingredient in any given meal and ask yourself what you could add to reduce the quantity of that ingredient without reducing the satisfaction of the dish. Nine times out of ten there's an answer.

Reducing Food Waste

Food waste is money in the bin. Every wilted vegetable, every leftover that gets forgotten at the back of the fridge, every heel of bread that goes stale — all of it represents money you've already spent that you're throwing away. Reducing waste is one of the quietest but most consistent ways to stretch your grocery budget further.

Use Every Part

Before anything goes in the bin, ask whether it has another use. Vegetable scraps — the ends of carrots, celery tops, onion skins, herb stems — can go into a freezer bag kept specifically for the purpose. When the bag is full, tip it all into a pot of water, simmer for an hour and you have a free vegetable stock that would otherwise have cost you nothing but would have cost money to buy. Chicken and meat bones do the same job — the carcass from your weekly roast chicken, boiled up with those frozen scraps, makes a stock that forms the base of soups, risottos and sauces throughout the week.

Anything that genuinely can't be eaten or used in the kitchen doesn't have to go to waste either. If you have chickens, most kitchen scraps make excellent feed — vegetable peelings, stale bread, leftover grains and pasta, the bits and pieces that didn't make it into a meal. Other pets can benefit from appropriate scraps too. And whatever is left after that goes to the compost, where it becomes something useful rather than just landfill.

The Leftover Platform

Leftovers have a habit of sitting in the fridge with good intentions and quietly turning into something nobody wants to eat three days later. The trick is building a leftover platform into your routine — a regular meal or time of day where using things up is the whole point.

For me that platform is breakfast. In our house everyone gets up at different times and breakfast is largely self serve — the rest of the family reach for their usuals without much thought. Weetbix, eggs on toast, cornflakes. Reliable, easy, done. But I use my breakfast as a fridge audit. A handful of cold chips from dinner the night before, reheated in a pan and served with a fried egg. Some leftover roasted vegetables from Sunday's roast, pan fried until they crisp up a little and topped with an egg. One lone rasher of bacon that's been sitting in the fridge, fried and folded into an omelet. One wrap left over from fajitas makes a base for a breakfast burrito. None of these are glamorous. All of them are genuinely good, cost almost nothing, and mean something gets used up rather than thrown away.

The egg is a recurring theme in my leftover breakfasts and for good reason — it's cheap (we have 'pet' chickens), it's protein, and it turns almost any leftover into something that feels like a proper meal rather than just yesterday's dinner reheated.

First In First Out

When you unpack your shopping, move older items to the front of the fridge and cupboards and put the new items behind them. It sounds simple because it is, but it's one of the most effective habits you can build. Things get used in the order they need to be used rather than sitting forgotten behind newer purchases until they're past saving.

The Wilting Vegetable Rule

When vegetables start to look a little tired, that's your signal to use them immediately rather than waiting another day. A slightly soft courgette, a bendy carrot, spinach that's starting to wilt — none of these are past it, they're just past their best raw. Cook them. A wilting vegetable soup, a stir fry, a frittata — these are the meals that use up what's left at the end of the week before the next shop arrives and cost you virtually nothing to make.

I always make the meals that use fresh vegetables or other ingredients first - so my shopping delivery is on a Tuesday - so Wednesday through Friday we dine on things like a side of steamed broccoli or cauliflower whilst at on Sunday/Monday we tend to have meals with less fresh items, if any at all like red lentil dahl or coconut chickpea curry.

Stale Bread

OK so our household doesn't tend to have too much stale bread because there are a lot of us and we bake almost daily. However stale bread is one of the most wasted items in Western households and one of the most versatile. Blitz it into breadcrumbs and freeze them for coating chicken or topping pasta bakes. Cube it and toast it in the oven for croutons. Soak it in egg and milk for a simple bread and butter pudding. Turn it into French toast for breakfast. There is almost no situation where stale bread needs to go in the bin.

Composting the things that genuinely can't be eaten closes the loop completely. Nothing goes to waste — it either gets eaten, feeds the animals, or goes back into the soil to grow more food.

Using Your Freezer

Your freezer is one of your most powerful frugal tools and it works hardest when you think of it as more than just a place to store frozen peas and ice cream. Used well it functions as a safety net, a preservation system, and an emergency pantry all at once.

Our freezer works across three distinct purposes and between them they cover almost every food waste and budget challenge we face.

1 - Freezing Leftovers and Odds and Ends

The first purpose is capturing things that would otherwise be wasted. Leftover pastry that didn't make it into a pie gets wrapped and frozen for a pie crust top another time. A stale bread roll goes in to wait for enough company before becoming a bread and butter pudding. A packet of mince gets divided into three portions — two for this week's meals, one for a week when the budget is tighter. The vegetable scrap bag lives in the freezer, growing steadily until it's ready for the stock pot. The stock itself, if it's not going to be used that week, gets poured into containers and frozen for later.

None of these are glamorous freezer moments. All of them represent money saved and waste avoided.

2 - Preserving Abundance

The second purpose is preservation. When you have more of something than you can use — a glut from the garden, a bulk buy on special, a harvest of roadside apples — the freezer is what bridges the gap between abundance now and need later. Cooked fruit fillings, homemade soups and sauces, bread, baked goods, blanched vegetables — most things freeze far better than people expect and having a well stocked freezer of homemade preserved food is one of the most satisfying frugal achievements there is.

3 - The Emergency Stockpile

The third purpose is the one that has genuinely saved us more times than I can count — the emergency stockpile. When the grocery budget is stretched thin, or an unexpected bill has eaten into what was earmarked for food, the answer is simple. You eat from the freezer. No big shop this week. Work through what you have, supplement with a small fresh shop for milk, bread and a few vegetables, and leave the freezer a little lighter than you found it.

I tend to have a few weeks a year — usually around birthday times when money is tightest — where we eat almost entirely from the freezer. A lot of homesteaders aim to do this for a full month, keeping a month's worth of supplies on hand at all times. I'm not a homesteader, I don't have the abundant vegetable garden, the freezer space or the forward planning for that, but even a week or two of eating from the freezer can make a significant difference when you need it to.

The freezer only works as a safety net if you treat it as one. That means being intentional about what goes in, labeling things clearly so you know what you have, and actually using what's in there rather than letting it become a graveyard of mystery containers and forgotten good intentions.

Batch Cooking

The principle behind batch cooking is simple — cook once, eat twice. Or three times. Or four. The idea is that when you're already in the kitchen with the oven on or a pot on the hob, a little extra effort produces a lot more food for very little additional cost or time. You're already there. You may as well make it count.

There's a real economy to it beyond just the food itself. Heating an oven costs money every single time you turn it on. If you're roasting a tray of vegetables for tonight's dinner, filling the rest of the oven with a second tray, a batch of muffins, or a pie costs you almost nothing extra in power because the oven is already at temperature. The same goes for hob cooking — a big pot of soup or bolognese uses barely more gas or electricity than a small one, but produces two or three times the meals. Batch cooking isn't just a food strategy, it's an energy strategy too.

The time saving compounds just as quickly. Chopping onions for one meal takes almost the same time as chopping onions for three. Washing up one large pot takes the same effort as washing up a small one. When you cook in volume you spread the labour across multiple meals and buy back time on the evenings when you need it most — the busy weeknights when the last thing you want to do is start from scratch.

Batch cooking doesn't have to mean spending an entire Sunday cooking twelve identical meals and stacking them in the freezer like a meal prep influencer. It can be as simple and unglamorous as doubling a bolognese recipe so half goes in the freezer, or making a full tray of roasted vegetables when you only need half of them tonight. The other half becomes tomorrow's frittata, next week's soup base, or a quick side dish that requires no effort at all.

We've already talked about the whole roast chicken — and that's perhaps the best example of batch cooking in action without it even feeling like batch cooking. One chicken, roasted once, becomes multiple meals across the week. The meat gets stripped and used in different dishes. The carcass becomes stock. The stock becomes soup or risotto. One cooking session, multiple outcomes, minimal waste. That's the whole principle right there.

The same logic applies across almost everything you cook. A big pot of chilli takes the same effort as a small one — so make a big one and eat it twice that week or freeze half. A tray of muffins costs almost the same in time and energy as a double batch — so make double and freeze the rest for school lunches. A soup that uses up the end of week vegetables can easily be made in a quantity that feeds you twice over.

Those bits and pieces that go into the freezer — the extra portion of bolognese, the leftover pie filling, the half bag of mince you divided up on a more abundant week — all of that becomes the buffer that carries you through the leaner weeks. Batch cooking and the freezer work together as a system. One feeds the other, and between them they give you a level of food security that a weekly shop alone can't provide...especially when every single week the price of groceries is increasing.

The key habits to build are simple. Always ask whether you can make more than you need right now. Always have freezer containers on hand so there's no barrier to putting something away. And always label what you freeze — a container of unidentified brown sauce is nobody's idea of a convenient weeknight dinner.

Mini Challenges

Even when you're already on a tight budget, there are times when money needs to be reallocated elsewhere — an unexpected bill, a school trip, a car repair that can't wait. When that happens, the grocery budget is often the only flexible line item you have left to work with. Mini challenges are a great way to squeeze a little more out of an already lean week, and as a bonus they break the monotony, give you a sense of achievement, and might just surprise you with what you're capable of.

1 - The $30 Challenge - Can you feed your family for $30 for the week? It sounds impossible but it's not — it just requires creativity and a willingness to eat simply for seven days. The idea isn't to go and spend $30 on a everything you need for the week, the idea is that you have $30 to supplement whatever you already have at home. The idea is to eat the things lurking in your fridge, freezer or pantry. It starts off reasonably easy - oh i have some bolognese in the freezer and some pasta in the pantry, that's the first night done. By night 7 you're dining on some typically odd combinations. It won't be your most delicious food week but it will prove to you that you can do far more with far less than you think.

2 - The No Spend Week - Spend nothing on food for a full week and eat only what you already have in the house. It's a brilliant way to clear out the freezer, use up forgotten pantry staples, and remind yourself how much food you actually have before you spend another cent. Most families are genuinely surprised by how long they can go. Again this challenge starts off easy and gets much harder as the week progresses.

3 - The No Spend Month A longer version of the same challenge — allow yourself one small shop for fresh essentials like milk and bread but otherwise eat from what you have. It requires more planning but the savings can be significant and satisfying. Imagine a whole month of grocery shops saved!

4 - Other Challenges There are plenty of other challenges that you can find online from meat free weeks where meat is switched out for cheaper protein options line eggs or legumes, to leftover week where every dinner is made from or repurposed from the night before.

We've done the $30 challenge more times than I can count — sometimes by choice, sometimes because something else needed that money more urgently. Either way it always reminds me that a full stomach doesn't require a full wallet and meal ingredients don't have to be conventionally paired.

Loyalty Schemes

When trying to manage the cost of groceries, loyalty schemes are genuinely worth engaging with — but only if you use them strategically. Used well they can deliver real savings and occasional treats that would otherwise be out of budget. Used poorly they become a sneaky way of spending more than you intended in pursuit of points you didn't need.

The golden rule of every loyalty scheme is this — it is only a saving if you were going to buy the item anyway. A bonus points offer on a product you don't normally buy is not an opportunity, it's a trap. The points are not worth more than the money you spent acquiring them.

Woolworths Everyday Rewards

The Woolworths Everyday Rewards programme is one of the most useful loyalty schemes available in New Zealand, particularly because of how broadly it connects — your points accumulate with your regular grocery shop and can also be earned at BP petrol stations among other places, which we will come back to in later chapters.

The key to making Woolworths Rewards work hard for you is understanding the bonus points offers. Each week there will be products offering extra points or multiplied points — sometimes four times, sometimes ten times the usual rate. If the product is something you buy regularly anyway, this is a genuine win. Stock up if the budget allows. If it's something you wouldn't normally buy, walk past it regardless of how appealing the points multiplier looks. You weren't going to buy it so you definitely don't need it.

The spend threshold offers work the same way — spend a certain amount on health and beauty products and earn significantly boosted points. If you need shampoo, conditioner, deodorant or other toiletries that week anyway, timing that purchase to coincide with a health and beauty bonus is smart shopping. If you're buying things you don't need just to hit the threshold, you've spent more than the points are worth.

For Woolworth's Everyday Rewards programme, 2000 points gets you a $15 voucher voucher. My own approach is to let my Woolworths rewards accumulate rather than spending them as they come in. Every year I hold onto them until mid November and then redeem the lot for Christmas. Nice biscuits, candy canes for the tree, the ingredients for my rocky road wreath dessert, the toppings for our Christmas Eve freaky sundaes — all the small luxuries that make Christmas feel special without blowing the budget. Twelve months of ordinary grocery shopping quietly funds a more generous festive table. It's one of my favourite frugal wins of the year. Just buy shopping 'normally' throughout the year I can easily accumulate $200-300 in rewards ready for Christmas.

New World

The New World operates on a similar principle — points accumulate with each shop and can be redeemed against future purchases. Check the current offers in store or via the app each week and apply the same logic as above. Bonus points on your usual buys are worth chasing. Bonus points that require you to change your shopping habits or spend more than planned are not.

Café Loyalty Cards

Most cafés offer some form of loyalty card — typically somewhere between five and ten coffees before you earn a free one. Petrol station cafés like Z and Wildbean at BP run them, chain stores like Night & Day, and most independent cafés offer something similar. If you're being truly frugal, buying coffee out isn't really on the cards — but if coffee is a non-negotiable in your life, at least make sure you're always getting your card stamped.

Getting Food for Free

Free food is out there if you know where to look and aren't too proud to take it. None of these options require much effort and some of them can make a genuinely meaningful difference to your weekly food budget.

1 - Neighbours and Community

Get to know your neighbours, particularly if they have fruit trees. A bag of lemons, a glut of feijoas, a box of apples from someone who can't use them all — these things are given away freely every single day by people who would rather see them used than rotting on the ground. A friendly relationship and a willingness to offer something in return — a loaf of homemade bread, some seedlings from your garden — goes a long way.

2 - Community Gardens and Orchards

Many towns and cities have community gardens and orchards where locals can get involved in exchange for a share of the produce. Turn up, do some weeding or planting, help tend the fruit trees, and benefit from what grows. It costs you nothing but a little time, gets you outside, and can supplement your fresh produce in a meaningful way. A quick search for community gardens and orchards in your area will tell you what's available locally.

3 - Community Pantries and Kai Cupboards

Community pantries — sometimes called Kai Cupboards — are a wonderful grassroots resource. Managed by local communities, they operate on a donate and take basis. People drop in non-perishable donations, or leave excess produce from their gardens — a glut of tomatoes, more courgettes than they know what to do with, a bag of onions. It's worth checking your local one whenever you happen to be passing. They are a little hit and miss depending on the day and what's been donated recently, so it's not worth going out of your way specifically — but as a casual stop when you're in the area they can add a few useful extras to your week for nothing.

4 - Foraging

Foraging is one of the oldest frugal skills there is and it's more accessible than most people realise. You don't need to live rurally or have specialist knowledge to get started — there are edible plants growing in hedgerows, riverbanks and roadsides in most parts of the country if you know what you're looking for.

Blackberry bushes are one of the most abundant and easy to identify — follow a river bank in late summer and you'll often find more than you can carry. Dandelion leaves are another easy starting point and are probably already in your garden, freely growing in the lawn, plentiful and surprisingly good in a summer salad. Stinging nettles, once blanched to remove the sting, make a flavoursome soup or can be used much like spinach. Wild apple trees, as we've already talked about, can produce a remarkable quantity of free fruit if you're in the right area.

I've foraged for blackberries, taken apples for trees growing at the side of the road, added dandelion leaves to salads through summer, and have used nettles in the past along with fern fronds. It connects you to the seasons and to your surroundings in a way that feels genuinely satisfying — and it's hard to beat the feeling of eating something that cost you nothing but a walk.

One important caveat — only forage for things you can confidently and correctly identify. If you're not certain, don't pick it. I don't touch mushrooms, for example, because I'm not confident enough in my identification to do so safely and the consequences of getting it wrong are not worth the risk. There are excellent foraging guides and apps available to help you learn, and a local foraging walk is a worthwhile small investment if you want to build your knowledge properly.

5 - Food Banks

Don't be ashamed to use a food bank. That's worth saying plainly because the shame around it is real and it stops people asking for help they genuinely need.

Food banks exist to help people in their time of need — and that includes you. Most don't have strict criteria around being on a benefit or earning under a specific income threshold. They are there for the weeks when an unexpected bill has derailed the budget, when work has been quiet, when your income simply won't stretch to cover enough food for your family that week. You don't need to be in crisis to ask for help. You just need to need it right now.

The first time I used a food bank I broke down and cried during the 'interview'. Not quietly in the car afterwards, but right there in front of a complete stranger during an open, frank conversation.It was the moment I had to acknowledge out loud to myself that due to a whole accumulation of circumstances I genuinely could not feed my family the way I wanted to. That was hard to sit with, I'm not from a family with open emotions, I'm British, we don't talk money. It wasn't particularly because of feeling like a failure that I cried but more due to the kindness and compassion I was being shown. Later, I thought about all the harvest festivals at school, all the Toot for Tucker drives I'd contributed to — all those tins I'd donated without a second thought to help 'those in need'. That goodwill had been sitting there waiting. This was simply my turn to receive it. And my turn to donate will come again.

Go. Ask. Accept the help without guilt.

Thank you to Michelle at the Salvation Army Food Bank — for your kindness, your compassion, and for never once making us feel judged. You made more of a difference than you know.

Paying It Forward

All of these free food resources — the community pantries, the food banks, the community gardens — exist because people donate to them. Donations of food, of time, of money. They rely entirely on the generosity of the community to keep going.

In the weeks and months when things are easier, remember that. Drop a few tins into the community pantry when you have a little extra. Donate a bag of groceries to the food bank at Christmas. Volunteer an hour at the community garden when you have the time but not the funds to donate. The same network that supports you in the hard times needs you to support it in the better ones. Pay it forward when you can.

The 14 day meal plan

Everything in this chapter, every single thing that I've learned keeping everyone fed over the years, comes together here. This is two real weeks of meals for a real family — built around a weekly grocery budget, two whole chickens, and every principle we've covered so far. You'll see meal planning in action, ingredients stretched and repurposed, batch cooking working in your favour, the freezer and stock pot earning their keep, and very little going to waste.

The week runs Wednesday to Tuesday because that's our shopping day. Tuesday is the day new groceries are introduced into our household — and that's an important point in itself. Build your meal plan around your own shopping day, not an arbitrary Monday start, and the whole week flows far more naturally. Towards the end of each week, as the fridge empties out and fresher foods have been consumed, the meals lean more heavily on pantry staples — and you'll notice that's exactly when our thriftiest meals come into action.

This isn't a rigid template to follow exactly (although you can if you'd like). It's an example of how all of this looks in practice, in a real kitchen, for a real family. Take what's useful, adapt it to your own tastes and budget, and use it as a starting point for building plans of your own.

WEEK ONE

WEDNESDAY

Breakfast: Porridge with cinnamon and brown sugar *(optional:*

grated apple if you have a glut, or a swirl of honey)

Lunch: Jacket potato with baked beans

Dinner: Roast your whole frozen chicken and separate out the portions - portion 1 is a breast, portion 2 is a breast, portion 3 is the legs and wings and portion 4 is a carcass.

Tonight you're utilising portion 1: a breast and using it to make an entire family meal with - Pesto Chicken Pasta.

Pop the carcass into your slow cooker or in a pot on the stove - you're making stock ready for tomorrow. If you're making your own bread, you need to make this too as you're using it for breakfast tomorrow!

THURSDAY

Breakfast: Eggs on toast

Lunch: Country Chicken Soup. Simply strain your overnight stock, add diced vegetables and the last scraps of chicken meat. A hearty, warming lunch that costs you almost nothing. Serve alone or add a side of bread.

Bulking tip: If you're needing/wanting to bulk it out, a handful or two of soup mix like yellow split peas and barley can create extra portions.

Dinner: Chicken Curry with Rice using portion 2: a breast from your roast chicken.

FRIDAY

Breakfast: Weetbix

Lunch: Jacket Potato with Chicken Curry

Dinner: Spaghetti Bolognese. Bulk generously with brown lentils. Let it simmer low and slow. Make double — you'll need the leftovers for Sunday's baked pasta dinner. Cook extra spaghetti tonight too and set it aside for tomorrow's lunch.

SATURDAY

Breakfast: Eggs on toast

Lunch: Spaghetti Fritters. Beat together eggs, cream and grated cheese. Stir through your leftover spaghetti and fry in spoonfuls until golden on both sides. A brilliant and surprisingly delicious use of last night's pasta.

Frugal tip: Can't afford cream this week? You can easily make this without.

Dinner: Red Lentil Dahl with Rice and Homemade Naan. Hearty, filling and simple. Make a double potion because you're eating this again for dinner on Tuesday.

SUNDAY

Breakfast: Porridge with cinnamon and sugar *(optional: grated apple or honey)*

Lunch: Jacket Potato with Baked Beans

Dinner: Bolognese Pasta Bake - repurpose the extra portion of bolognese you made on Friday, stir through cooked pasta, top with cheese and bake until golden.

MONDAY

Breakfast: Weetbix

Lunch: Country Chicken Soup *(yes, you're still eating the soup you made on Thursday)*

Dinner: Potato Bake. A simple, comforting bake of sliced potatoes, onion and cheese. Add any remaining chicken scraps or vegetables if you have them.

TUESDAY — SHOPPING DAY

Breakfast: Eggs on toast

Lunch: Jacket Potato with Baked Beans or any left over portions of anything from previous days.

Dinner: Red Lentil Dahl with Rice and Homemade Flatbread

WEEK TWO

WEDNESDAY

Breakfast: Porridge with cinnamon and sugar *(optional: grated apple or honey)*

Lunch: Cheese and tomato omelet

Frugal tip: No tomatoes? Just make it a cheese omelette. Got some zucchini from a garden glut? Turn it into a cheese and zucchini omelette.

Dinner: Roast your whole frozen chicken and separate out the portions as per last week - portion 1 is a breast, portion 2 is a breast, portion 3 is the legs and wings and portion 4 is a carcass.

Tonight you're utilising portion 3: the legs. You'll also need the legs from last week's chicken too. Dinner is Chicken Legs with roast vegetables and yorkshire puddings served with gravy.

Make plenty of vegetables because the leftovers are utilised for breakfast tomorrow.

And don't forget to pop that carcass in the slow cooker, it's soup time tomorrow.

Bulk cooking tip: You only need one yorkshire pudding per family member but most recipes easily make the full 12 a cake tin holds so make the full batch, cook and freeze the extra yorkshire pudding for another week.

THURSDAY

Breakfast: Leftover roasted vegetables pan fried and topped with a fried egg

Lunch: Chicken Noodle Soup

Strain your overnight stock, add noodles and a can of corn. Light, warming and delicious. Serve with some fresh bread or a bread roll to bulk it out.

Dinner: Red Thai Chicken Curry with Rice

You're using one of the breasts from your roasted chicken to create this dish. Add cubed boiled potatoes and carrots and stir through a red thai curry sauce and coconut cream. Serve with rice.

FRIDAY

Breakfast: Weetbix

Lunch: Chicken Noodle Soup

Second round of noodle soup.

Bulking tip: Add a handful of extra noodles or vegetables to bulk it out.

Dinner: Chilli and Rice

You're using your tray of mince and bulking generously with black beans, kidney beans and tinned tomatoes. Make double — the leftovers become Sunday's burritos. Serve tonight over rice.

Make a double batch of rice too as we're going to use it for tomorrow's dinner.

SATURDAY

Breakfast: Eggs on toast

Lunch: Jacket potato with leftover chilli

Dinner: Chicken Fried Rice

You're using the second portion of chicken breast from your roast chicken. Fry the chicken breast with the rice from yesterday, frozen peas, egg, soy sauce, garlic and ginger and any extra vegetables you have on hand. A fast, cheap and genuinely satisfying dinner with very little effort.

SUNDAY

Breakfast: Porridge with honey

Lunch: Cheese and onion frittata - add a handful of spinach if you have it.

Dinner: Burritos

Remember that double batch of chilli you made earlier this week? You're using it today. Simply warm it through and serve wrapped in flatbreads with grated cheese, sour cream if the budget allows, and whatever salad ingredients you have on hand. Same base as Friday's chilli — completely different meal.

MONDAY

Breakfast: Weetbix

Lunch: Chicken Noodle Soup

Yes again, at this point it's probably more noodle and essence of chicken but it's still a delicious lunch which can be served with bread or croutons to bulk it out. Drizzle through an egg on reheating and a splash of soy sauce and it gives it a subtle asian twist.

Dinner: Creamy Coconut Chickpea Curry

A delicious coconut base with chickpeas for a protein punch. Perfect for the day before grocery shopping as it doesn't use any fresh ingredients. Although if you happen to have any cauliflower hanging around in your fridge, it makes a great addition.

Save some for tomorrow's lunch!

Tuesday

Breakfast: Poached eggs on toast

Lunch: Creamy coconut chickpea curry

Dinner: Pot Pie

So this meal is planned around whatever cheap meat you managed to grab during your grocery shop - sliced ham, bacon pieces, mince (you can hold some back from cooking your chilli), you're making a vegetable based pie with a handful of meat and gravy. Then either top with mashed potato or make a quick pastry top for it.

Handy hint - if fish is available and affordable, you can switch this out for a creamy fish pie - it works with either the mashed potato top or pastry on.

3

Keeping the Lights On

After groceries, power is one of the biggest controllable costs in most households — and unlike rent or mortgage payments, there's genuinely a lot you can do to bring it down. This chapter covers everything from choosing the right plan and provider, through to the small daily habits that add up to real savings over a year.

Comparing Electricity Companies

Before you even think about changing your habits, make sure you're not simply paying too much for the same electricity everyone else gets. Switching providers is free, doesn't involve any physical changes to your home, and can be one of the single biggest savings you make with almost no ongoing effort.

Start by working out roughly how many kWh your household uses each month — this will be on your power bill, usually as a monthly or daily average. Once you know that number, you can properly compare plans rather than just looking at headline prices.

Every plan has two components — a daily fixed charge and a per kWh variable charge. A plan with a low daily charge but a high kWh rate might suit a low usage household, while a plan with a higher daily charge but cheaper kWh rate often works out better for a larger family using more power. Run your actual usage through both and see which comes out cheaper — don't assume.

One important catch to watch for — make sure you're comparing like for like when it comes to GST. Some providers display their rates excluding GST, others include it. You will be paying GST either way, so if you're comparing a rate that looks cheap against one that looks more expensive, check whether one of them simply hasn't added the 15% yet. Always compare GST inclusive figures, or you may end up choosing the more expensive plan by accident.

It's also worth checking whether you qualify as a "low user." Under current regulations, a low user is a household using less than 8,000 kWh per year (slightly higher in parts of the South Island), and low user plans cap the daily fixed charge but charge more per kWh. If your usage is genuinely low, this can work in your favour — if it's not, a standard plan with a higher fixed charge but lower per kWh rate may end up cheaper overall.

Beyond the basic plan structure, look at what each provider offers in terms of free or discounted power periods. Some offer free power on weekends, others free hours overnight or in the evening. If your household's usage genuinely lines up with those free periods — running the washing machine, dishwasher or dryer overnight for example — these plans can make a real difference.

My husband and I once had a fairly serious conversation about whether we could realistically turn our entire household nocturnal to make the most of a free overnight power deal. We were working from home, the kids were doing correspondence school with no set hours - it was theoretically possible - breakfast at 7pm, lunch at midnight, dinner at 6am - all the household electricity use between. We decided against it — mostly because neither of us could face being awake at those hours on a regular basis — but it's testament to how tempting those free periods can be once you start doing the maths....or how desperate we were to cut costs at the time.

Reducing Electricity Use in the Kitchen

The kitchen is one of the biggest power users in any home, largely because of the oven, the hob, and the fridge and freezer running around the clock. A few habits make a real difference here.

Batch cooking, which we covered in the Keeping Everyone Fed chapter, applies just as much to power as it does to food. If the oven is on, make the most of it — cook multiple things at once rather than heating it up again later for a single item.

If you have a benchtop oven or an air fryer, use it instead of your full sized oven whenever you're cooking something small. A full oven uses considerably more power to heat up and maintain temperature than a smaller appliance does, so save the big oven for when you're genuinely using the space.

Keep your fridge and freezer full. A full fridge or freezer retains cold more efficiently than an empty one, meaning the compressor doesn't have to work as hard or as often. If you don't have enough food to fill the space, bottles of tap water do the job just as well. As a bonus, this doubles as a small emergency water stockpile — handy in a power cut or any other situation where your water supply is interrupted.

When you boil the kettle, boil a little extra and pour it into a thermos. That way if you want another hot drink later in the day, or need hot water for cooking, it's already there without reboiling.

A few other kitchen habits worth building in — only boil as much water as you actually need rather than filling the kettle every time, use lids on pots to retain heat and cook faster, and if you have a dishwasher, only run it when it's full and use the eco setting if it has one. Although in our household we actually do all the washing up ourselves for two reasons: the first is habit, we lived off grid for a long time, then in a home without a dishwasher so it become habit, secondly I can't bring myself to buy those overpriced dishwasher tablets when some cheap dishwashing liquid does the job for a fraction of the price, and a fraction of the water!

Reducing Hot Water Cylinder Costs

Heating water is one of the most expensive things your power does, day in and day out, whether you're using it or not. A couple of straightforward changes can reduce that cost meaningfully.

Check your cylinder's thermostat — many are set higher than necessary. Around 60 degrees is generally considered the sweet spot, hot enough to be safe and effective but not wastefully hot.

If your cylinder isn't already insulated, a cylinder wrap is a small, one-off cost that pays for itself quickly by reducing the amount of heat lost while the water sits waiting to be used. Can't afford a cylinder wrap? Get creative, wrap a blanket around it or some left over insulation battens.

Shorter showers make a genuinely significant difference over time — cutting shower time down by even a few minutes per person per day adds up considerably across a week, a month, and a year. A low flow shower head is a small investment that reduces hot water use every single time it's used, without anyone really noticing the difference. Or simply shower less often. There is no need to shower every single day. During our off-grid years, we only set the outdoor shower up in summer, during the winter we used a bowl of water and wash cloths to keep clean or utilised showers elsewhere - your local swimming pool has showers, if you're the member of a gym you can shower there or if you live in a tourist area, public toilets sometimes have shower facilities (especially near beaches or lakes).

For those paying water charges through a water meter, using less water for showering will significantly reduce your water rates too.

Charging Devices Away From Home

It sounds like a small thing, but charging phones, tablets and laptops away from home rather than constantly topping them up on your own power adds up, particularly if you're trying to make the most of free or discounted power periods or low user rates.

USB charging points are everywhere now — the library, cafés, the car. If you're out and about during the day, or even if you're at work, take the opportunity to top up devices while you're there rather than the moment you get home. I even keep a laptop charger in the car, which has been genuinely useful on longer trips.

Power banks are another simple solution — charge them anywhere convenient for free, then use them at home to charge your devices without drawing directly from your household power at all.

You can also get solar chargers or generators if you want to go down that route but the initial outlay is quite high and it could therefore take years to recoup that cost through your electric bills.

Heat Pumps and Keeping Warm

Heat pumps are one of the most efficient ways to heat a home, but how you use one makes a big difference to your power bill. The most effective approach is to heat the room you're actually in, with the door closed, rather than trying to heat the whole house. An empty bedroom doesn't need to be the same temperature as the living room you're sitting in all evening. I once read a book about a family who, every winter, closed up most of their house entirely (like literally boarded it up) and lived almost exclusively in one room — eating, relaxing, and even sleeping there — so that only that single room needed heating. It's an extreme example, but the principle behind it is sound. The fewer spaces you heat, the less it costs.

Set your heat pump to a sensible temperature — around 18 to 20 degrees is generally considered comfortable and efficient — rather than cranking it up high and then turning it off when it gets too warm. A steady, moderate temperature uses less power overall than constant on-off cycling at a higher setting.

Beyond the heat pump itself, heating yourself rather than the space around you is one of the oldest frugal tricks there is, and it still works. Extra layers, a beanie indoors, thick socks, a jumper, a lap blanket on the couch — all of these mean you're comfortable at a lower room temperature. A hot water bottle in bed means you don't need the heater running into the evening. There are also battery powered heated gilets and vests now, charged via USB or a power bank, which some people swear by for keeping warm during the day without heating a room at all. I haven't taken the plunge on one myself — the upfront cost gives me pause — but I like the principle, and if you can pick one up secondhand or on sale it's worth considering.

If you heat your home with a log burner rather than a heat pump, the same principle applies — the less you pay for fuel, the lower your heating costs. Firewood can be expensive to buy in bulk, but there are ways to reduce that cost significantly if you're willing to put in a little effort.

Pine cones make excellent kindling and cost nothing — a walk in the right area will fill a bag quickly and they catch and burn beautifully to get a fire going. Wood offcuts from building sites, timber yards or local tradespeople are often available free or very cheaply, and broken wooden pallets are similarly easy to come by — many businesses are happy for someone to take them off their hands. Both burn well and can significantly reduce how much bought firewood you get through in a season.

If you live near a beach, driftwood is another free option that washes up in useful quantities, particularly after a storm. Once dry, it burns well and costs nothing but the time to collect it. One important caveat however — do not burn driftwood in a wetback system. We learned this the hard way. The salt content in driftwood corrodes the pipes over time and the repair bill is considerably more painful than the saving was ever worth.

When I was growing up in the UK, we had central heating via radiators. My parents religiously turned them on in October and off again in May, regardless of the actual outdoor temperature or weather. The timer heated the house in the early morning and late evening, the thermostat was set low and you were forbidden from touching it. I remember a chilly childhood, so does my husband but I guess our parents were running on a budget too. Turns out frugal living has been around a lot longer than the hashtag.

A Few More Quick Wins

A handful of other small changes are worth building into your routine:

- Switching to LED bulbs throughout the house is one of the cheapest upgrades you can make and pays for itself quickly in reduced lighting costs.
- Make sure your curtains are thermal backed and reach the floor. Close them once it starts getting dark — this alone makes a noticeable difference to how much heat a room retains. Curtains are expensive, especially good quality ones so look to local Op Shops or second hand stores, look out for sales or contact your local curtain bank who can help low income families with thermal curtains - you don't get to choose the style or colour but regardless, they'll help keep your home warm.
- Turn appliances off at the wall rather than leaving them on standby, particularly anything with a display clock or light, as these draw power continuously even when not in use.
- If you're due to replace an appliance like a fridge, washing machine or dryer, choose the most energy efficient option

you can afford — older inefficient appliances can cost significantly more to run every single year, and that difference compounds over the life of the appliance.

4

Keeping a Roof Over Your Head

How you keep this cost down depends largely on whether you rent or own your home — the levers available to you are quite different. For renters, it's about choosing the right property and the right area. For homeowners, it's about the mortgage itself — how much you borrowed, what rate you're on, and how quickly you're working towards paying it off.

The ultimate dream for most people is a fully paid off home with no mortgage at all. It's a genuinely achievable goal for some, and one that we have always been told is worth working towards. But it's worth saying clearly — even a freehold home isn't free. Council rates and insurance continue regardless of whether you owe the bank anything, and those costs only tend to go in one direction. Owning your home outright removes your biggest expense, but it doesn't remove housing costs altogether.

Size Matters

Whether you're renting or buying, a smaller home costs less. This is true at almost every level — the purchase price or rent is lower, the rates are typically lower, insurance is cheaper, and a smaller space is considerably easier and cheaper to heat. It's also easier to maintain — less roof, less guttering, typically less garden, less to clean and less to repair when something goes wrong. So choose the size of your home wisely.

Does Everyone Need Their Own Room?

One of the biggest drivers of "needing" a bigger home is the assumption that every child needs their own bedroom. If you have three children, the instinct is often to look for a four bedroom home — one for the adults, and one each for the kids. But this is a relatively modern, Western expectation, and it's worth questioning whether it's actually necessary for your family.

We lived in a one bedroom tiny home for three years when our older two children were six and eight. They shared a room the entire time. Initially they shared with us, a double bed and a set of bunks crammed into the smallest space possible - everyone had one drawer of a dresser to keep their clothing in. Eventually the kids moved into a separate sleepout, where they continued to share — even once they were eight and eleven. It was never an issue, and they are not even the same gender. They don't even particularly like each other. They had their own bunks and their own spaces within the room. Sharing a room isn't a hardship — for a lot of kids it's genuinely enjoyable, and it's far more normal in many parts of the world than the one-child-one-room model

New Zealand and similar countries have come to expect.

Before assuming you need more bedrooms than you currently have, think honestly about whether your children would genuinely struggle sharing, or whether it's simply an assumption nobody has questioned.

Choosing Where You Live

Location has a huge impact on housing costs. Rentals and house prices in major centres — particularly Auckland and Wellington — are significantly higher than in regional New Zealand. Moving even an hour or two out of a major centre can mean a substantially lower rent or mortgage for a comparable or even larger property.

The trade-off, of course, is often commuting. It's worth genuinely weighing this up rather than assuming a cheaper rural property is automatically the better deal. Calculate the actual cost of commuting — fuel, vehicle wear and tear, parking — and compare that against the savings on rent or mortgage. Don't forget to factor in your time too. A cheaper home that adds two hours of commuting to your day has a cost beyond money, and only you can decide whether that trade-off is worth it for your family.

Sharing Costs — Flatting and Boarders

One of the simplest ways to bring housing costs down is to share them. Flatting — splitting a rental between unrelated adults — is extremely common in New Zealand, particularly among younger people, but there's no reason it has to stop once you have a family or a mortgage. Splitting rent, rates, insurance and utilities across more people means everyone's individual share is smaller, often dramatically so.

If you own your home and have a spare room, taking in a boarder is worth genuinely considering. A boarder's contribution can take real pressure off a mortgage payment, and depending on your arrangement may also help cover a share of power, internet and rates. It does mean sharing your space with someone outside your immediate family, which isn't the right fit for everyone — but for those who are comfortable with it, it can be one of the most financially impactful decisions a homeowner makes.

Multi-Generational Living

A related but quite different option is multi-generational living — parents, adult children, grandparents, or extended family sharing a home together, often across multiple generations under one roof. This isn't a new idea by any means; it's how many families lived for generations before the expectation became that every adult, couple or family unit should have their own separate home. In many cultures it remains entirely normal.

The financial benefits can be significant. Housing costs, whether that's rent, a mortgage, rates or insurance, are shared across more adults. Grocery shops can be done in bulk for a larger household, often working out cheaper per person. Childcare costs can disappear entirely if grandparents are on hand and willing. In return, older family members may receive support, company, and help around the home as they age.

It's not without its challenges — different households have different habits, routines and expectations, and it requires a genuine willingness from everyone involved to make it work. But for families who get on well and are open to it, multi-generational living can solve a housing cost problem and a care problem at the same time, and many families find the lifestyle benefits go well beyond the financial ones.

Renting Out What You're Not Using

If you have a spare room, a sleepout, or even just a house that sits empty while you're away, there may be an opportunity to earn a little income from it. Platforms like Airbnb or Bookabach let you list a space short term, even just occasionally — over a holiday period, or a weekend away. It won't replace an income but it can take the edge off a power bill or rates payment for the month.

Reviewing Your Mortgage Regularly

If you have a mortgage, it shouldn't be something you set up once and forget about for the next twenty or thirty years. Interest rates change, lenders change their offers, and loyalty to your bank is not rewarded the way you might assume.

A mortgage broker is worth using and costs you nothing directly — they're paid by the lender, not by you. A good broker has access to deals across multiple lenders and can do the legwork of shopping around on your behalf, something most people simply don't have the time or inclination to do themselves.

It's also worth understanding the difference between fixed and variable (floating) rates, and not assuming one is always better than the other. Fixed rates give you certainty for a set period. Variable rates can move with the market — sometimes in your favour, sometimes not. Many people split their mortgage between fixed and variable portions to hedge their bets.

Don't be loyal out of habit. Just because your everyday banking is with one bank doesn't mean your mortgage needs to be with the same one. Just because you've been with a particular lender for ten years doesn't mean you can't switch now if a better deal is available elsewhere. Review your mortgage at every renewal, and don't be afraid to move it if the numbers work out better elsewhere.

Borrow Less, Pay It Off Faster

When taking out a mortgage, borrow the bare minimum you can manage — not the maximum the bank is willing to lend you. Just because you're approved for a certain amount doesn't mean you should take all of it, in fact you probably shouldn't. A smaller mortgage means less interest over the life of the loan and more breathing room in your budget every fortnight.

Once you have a mortgage, look for ways to pay it off faster. Regular overpayments, even small ones, make a real difference over time — an extra $10 per pay cycle might not feel like much, but compounded over years it can shave months off the end of your mortgage term and save you a meaningful amount in interest. If your lender allows lump sum payments without penalty, putting any windfalls — tax refunds, bonuses, gifts — towards the mortgage rather than spending them does the same job on a larger scale.

When choosing your mortgage term, consider shorter options where realistic. A 30 year term keeps your payments lower but costs considerably more in interest over the life of the loan. If your budget can handle it, a 20 or even 10 year term means higher regular payments but a dramatically reduced total cost — and a much earlier date for becoming mortgage free.

First Home Buyer Support

If home ownership is the goal, it's worth looking into what government support exists for first home buyers — KiwiSaver first home withdrawal schemes and any first home grants currently available can make a meaningful difference to a deposit. These schemes change over time, so it's worth checking current eligibility directly rather than relying on what was available a few years ago.

Struggling With Housing Costs

If you're a renter and genuinely struggling to keep up, it's worth knowing that financial support such as the Accommodation Supplement exists through Work and Income for those who qualify. As with the food bank conversation earlier in this book — there's no shame in checking whether you're eligible for support that exists specifically to help in situations like this.

Living Outside the Box — Our Garage Years

I mentioned earlier in this book that during our off grid years in Hokitika we built a garage and lived in it. I want to expand on that a little here because it's directly relevant to this chapter — for three years, it meant we had no rent and no mortgage at all.

To be completely transparent, it wasn't a tiny home in the polished, Pinterest sense of the word. It was, quite literally, a garage. We insulated it ourselves and divided it with internal walls into a car space, a living area and a bedroom. Were we legally allowed to live there long term? No. Did we do it anyway? Yes.

I'm not going to pretend that's a solution for everyone, or that I'd recommend it without caveats — there are genuine legal and safety considerations to think about with this kind of arrangement, and it won't suit every family, every climate, or every stage of life. But I'd be doing this book a disservice if I left it out, because the financial impact was enormous.

A typical rental in our area at the time was around $350 a week. For three years, we didn't pay that. Not once. Three years at $350 a week comes to well over $50,000 in rent we simply didn't have to find. That's not a small saving — that's life changing money, and it's a huge part of how we later became mortgage free (at least for a while) - investing in land improvements in one property to then sell at a higher price and buy elsewhere.

We're back renting now, and there's a different kind of saving in that too, at least in the short term. After a recent relocation for work, our house is on the market and we actually don't plan to replace it any time soon. Why? Because we want a break from the rates bills and home insurance premiums that land monthly. We also want to break from the maintenance costs owning a property involves. One set rent, every fortnight with no rates or insurance and no unexpected bills to fix things - there's currently relief in that prospect for us. Depending on your situation, particularly if you're between properties or in a temporary living situation, renting can actually work out better on a short term basis once you account for those costs that homeowners often forget to factor in.

The broader point is this — housing is the area where the most unconventional solutions often produce the biggest savings. A garage, a sleepout, a converted shed, living with family for a period, house-sitting between properties — none of these are the "normal" path, and none of them are forever. But if your goal is to get ahead financially, sometimes the biggest lever you can pull is being willing to live somewhere, or some way, that doesn't look like everyone else's version of normal for a while.

5

Keeping You Moving

After housing, food and utilities, transport is often the next biggest line item in a family budget — and it's an area where costs can creep up almost invisibly. Fuel, registration, insurance, servicing, repairs, depreciation — it all adds up, and a vehicle that felt affordable when you bought it can become a genuine drain if you're not paying attention. This chapter is about getting from A to B without it costing more than it needs to.

Buying Second Hand

A car is not an investment. The moment you drive a new car off the forecourt it has already lost a significant chunk of its value, and that depreciation continues steeply for the first few years of its life. Buying second hand means someone else has already absorbed that initial hit, and you're paying a price that reflects the car's actual ongoing value far more closely.

This doesn't mean buying the cheapest, oldest car you can find and hoping for the best. It means buying within your means, doing your research, and prioritising reliability over appearance.

A slightly older, well maintained, commonly available model — the kind with parts that are easy and cheap to source and mechanics who know it well — will almost always serve a family better than something flashier that turns out to be expensive or difficult to keep on the road.

Do You Need Two Cars?

For many families, two vehicles feels like a given — one for each adult, plus the logistics of school runs, activities and appointments. But it's worth genuinely asking whether your family could manage on one and what that would look like.

Running a second car isn't just the purchase price. It's a second registration, a second insurance policy, a second WOF, second set of tyres, and all the servicing and maintenance that comes with it — on top of an asset that's depreciating the whole time, often while sitting in the driveway unused for large parts of the day. Dropping to one car requires more coordination — shared schedules, walking or cycling for some trips, staying home or occasionally relying on others — but for some families the savings are substantial enough to make that coordination well worth it.

I grew up in a one car household. My father used it for work every day, and the rest of life simply happened around that. I walked to the greengrocer, the deli and the butcher with my mum. I walked to the park, walked to school. My mother walked to work too, right up until she retired. The big grocery shop was done once a month, using the car, timed around payday — everything else was on foot or on a bus for something further afield. My mother didn't particularly enjoy driving anyway, and we lived somewhere walkable enough that she rarely needed to. It was the eighties and nineties, and plenty of households around us were the same. I didn't know any different, and it never felt like we were missing out.

Fast forward to my life in New Zealand, and that model simply doesn't translate the way it once did. Unless you're living right in a major centre, or in the heart of a small town, a car becomes close to essential. Public transport is sparse outside the main cities, and even where it exists it often doesn't run frequently enough to build a daily routine around. Footpaths themselves can be sparse too — plenty of rural and semi-rural roads have no pedestrian provision at all, which makes walking to the shops or to school simply not viable, let alone safe. The geography here is so different — properties are bigger, distances between amenities are greater, and towns are often spread out in a way that assumes everyone has a car.

It's a good reminder that what works for reducing transport costs depends enormously on where you live. The walkable, one car childhood I had in the UK isn't really an option for most people here — but understanding why it worked there can still help you think about which trips genuinely need the car and which don't, even if the car itself isn't optional.

Reducing Fuel Costs

How you drive has a real impact on how much fuel you use. Smooth, gradual acceleration and braking uses considerably less fuel than constant speeding up and slowing down. Keeping your tyres at the correct pressure improves fuel efficiency — under-inflated tyres create more rolling resistance and burn more fuel. Removing roof racks or roof boxes when they're not in use reduces drag, and an overloaded car uses more fuel than one carrying only what it needs to.

Combining errands into a single trip rather than multiple short journeys throughout the week also makes a real difference. A cold engine uses more fuel in its first few minutes than a warm one, so four separate short trips will use considerably more fuel than the same total distance covered in one trip with a warm engine throughout.

It's also worth knowing where fuel is cheapest. Apps like Gaspy let you check prices at stations near you before you fill up, and prices can vary more than people expect between stations just a few minutes apart. If your supermarket loyalty program offers a fuel discount through an affiliated petrol station — as we discussed with Woolworths Rewards and BP in a previous chapter — make sure you're using it. It's also worth being aware of which petrol stations have discounts on which days, for example for NPD its Thursday. The only thing to be aware of is using extra petrol to get to a petrol station that is offering a discount or reward points if it's not on your way to somewhere else, you're actually using extra fuel and it can be counter productive in your savings.

Maintenance — Little and Often

Regular servicing might feel like an expense you could put off, but a well maintained car is a reliable car, and reliability is what keeps the bigger, more expensive repairs at bay. Small issues caught early are almost always cheaper to fix than the same issue left until it causes a bigger problem.

There's also a lot you can do yourself, with no mechanical knowledge required. Checking your oil level, tyre pressure, and topping up windscreen washer fluid takes minutes and costs nothing. Replacing wiper blades yourself rather than paying a garage to do it is a small saving that adds up. Keeping an eye on tyre tread and getting them rotated regularly extends their life and delays one of the more expensive routine costs of car ownership.

In my younger years I just thought my car would run and run forever. It wasn't until I met my husband, a former mechanic, that I truly understood the need to look after my car. Thankfully he does most of the 'looking after' for me but the principle is understood.

Alternatives to Driving

Not every trip needs to be made by car. Walking or cycling for short local trips — to school, to a nearby shop, to a friend's house — costs nothing, has obvious health benefits, and reduces wear on your vehicle and your fuel bill at the same time.

Where public transport is available and practical, it's worth considering for regular trips like commuting to work. Even using it occasionally, on days when it makes sense, reduces your overall fuel use and vehicle wear over the year.

Carpooling is another option worth exploring, particularly for school runs or commutes where other families or colleagues are travelling the same route at the same time. Splitting the driving, or splitting the fuel cost, benefits everyone involved.

I appreciate these options might not be available to everyone, depending on where you live but if they are available, a simple change can save some money.

Insurance – Shop Around Annually

The same principle that applies to your mortgage and your power company applies to your car insurance — don't assume your current provider is still offering you the best deal just because they did when you first signed up. Get quotes from a few providers each year at renewal time and don't be afraid to switch if a better deal is available elsewhere.

It's also worth considering whether comprehensive cover is genuinely necessary for every vehicle in your household. For an older car worth a relatively small amount, third party cover might be more appropriate and considerably cheaper, while a newer or more valuable vehicle may justify the cost of comprehensive cover. There's no one right answer — it depends on what the vehicle is actually worth and what you could realistically afford to replace or repair it for if something happened.

One thing that I will always pay extra for is windscreen cover. I've lost count on the number of times a stone has been flung up and either chipped or cracked my windscreen whilst living in New Zealand. Some things that you might think are a saving, like not getting the extra cover, can result in a higher repair cost later on.

The Real Cost of a Car

When working out whether a vehicle is affordable, it's easy to focus only on the purchase price or the weekly fuel spend and forget everything else that comes with it. Registration, insurance, WOF, servicing, tyres, road user charges and depreciation all need to be factored in alongside fuel to understand what a car genuinely costs you to own over a year, not just to drive.

Looking at the full picture like this can be eye opening — and it's often what makes the case for a smaller, simpler, more reliable vehicle, or for seriously considering whether your household needs one car or two, all the clearer.

6

Keeping Up Appearances

Looking after how you present yourself doesn't have to come with a hefty price tag. Clothing, hair, nails and makeup are all areas where spending tends to creep up gradually, driven more by habit and trend than by genuine need. This chapter is about stepping back from that and asking what you actually need to look and feel like yourself, rather than what you've been conditioned to think you need to buy.

How Many Outfits Do You Actually Need?

When we lived in our tiny home, each of us had four outfits and seven sets of underwear — enough to fit in one allocated drawer. We did laundry weekly, in town, and it worked. That said, it wouldn't have worked for my now messy toddler, who realistically needed more than a once a week wash, but we didn't have her at the time.

Now that we're a bigger family, laundry happens daily rather than weekly — but the principle hasn't really changed. My teenagers reach for the same couple of outfits over and over, regardless of how much else is in their wardrobe. If I'm honest, so do I. Most of us have favourites, and most of us wear a small rotation of those favourites far more often than anything else we own. The rest tends to just sit there. So instead of buying more, look to your own wardrobe and start putting together outfits from it and wear them.

Footwear

You don't need a different pair of shoes for every occasion. A small, practical collection covers almost everything most families need — gumboots or wellingtons for wet weather and outdoor jobs, jandals, sandals or crocs for summer and quick trips, trainers for everyday wear and activity, and a pair of boots for anything that needs a bit more warmth or durability. Beyond that, most additional pairs are more about variety than necessity.

Where to Buy

Op shops and charity shops are genuinely worth your time, particularly for kids' clothing which gets outgrown long before it's worn out. Trade Me and Designer Wardrobe are excellent for picking up specific brands or better quality pieces secondhand, often at a fraction of the retail cost. Buy and sell groups on Facebook are particularly good for searching out specific items like merino layers or well known outdoor brands, which hold their value and their quality well secondhand. You can often buy bulk lots for the kids too, helping keep them clothed seasonally.

It's worth being cautious of ultra cheap fast fashion sites like Shein and Temu. I've ordered from Temu myself and the reality rarely matches the photos — tops in thin, shiny synthetic fabrics that don't look or feel like the image, and everything seemingly cut cropped regardless of what was actually pictured. It might feel like a bargain at the time, but if it doesn't fit properly, doesn't last, and ends up unworn or thrown out within months, it wasn't actually cheap at all. That's false economy — money spent for nothing.

If you have younger children coming up behind older siblings, hang onto good quality clothing as it's outgrown. Op shop quality basics and brand name pieces that have plenty of life left in them are worth storing away rather than donating immediately, especially if there's a sibling who'll fit into them in a year or two.

The Art of Wearing Your Clothes Out

You don't need four pairs of jeans on rotation. You need a pair of jeans — and when they wear out, you replace them. If you're starting from a fairly full wardrobe right now, there's a good chance you already own enough to see you through years of normal wear without buying anything new at all. The goal isn't to never buy clothes again, it's to buy when something is genuinely worn out, not when you're simply bored of what you have.

Mending extends that further still. A small hole, a popped seam, a worn knee — these don't have to mean the end of an item's life. When my son was little and constantly on his hands and knees, I patched the knees of his trousers over and over, right up until he was about six. A patch on the knee of a toddler's trousers isn't a flaw, it's just visible proof that the trousers are still doing their job.

Accessories

Accessories are one area where buying fewer, better pieces genuinely pays off, because the right pieces go with everything and last indefinitely. My own everyday jewellery is a small handful of pieces I've worn for years — a chain with a cross and a symbol that has meaning to me, a pair of silver hoop earrings, and a chunky turquoise necklace my husband bought me on a trip to the Maldives, long before we had kids. None of them are trend pieces. All of them go with almost anything I wear, and none of them have ever gone out of style because they were never "in" style to begin with — they're just mine.

The same logic applies to bags. One everyday bag that's practical and durable, and one for evenings or occasions when you need it, is genuinely enough for most people. Beyond that, most additional bags spend more time in a cupboard than on your shoulder.

Hair

A regular wash, cut and colour at a hairdresser can easily run into hundreds of dollars, and for many people it's a recurring cost every few weeks. There are several ways to bring this right down without giving up looking after yourself.

The simplest is to leave more time between cuts, or have a trusted friend or family member trim your hair at home. A basic trim doesn't require professional training to do safely, particularly for styles that don't need precision.

If you do need a hairdresser, wash your hair yourself before you go and ask for just the cut — skip the wash, blow dry and styling that usually comes bundled with it. Many salons will charge less for a cut only appointment, and you'll get the same result for less money.

Colouring is one of the biggest ongoing hair costs, and there are really two paths here — colour it yourself at home with box dye, or embrace your natural colour entirely.

I have a story on this one. I'd always done my own home dye without any issues. Then one of the kids got headlice. So did I. The headlice treatment completely ruined my hair colour — I ended up with a horrific orange. A hairdresser took one look and told me the only sensible option was to cut it short and grow out my natural colour. Turns out, in my late thirties, my natural colour was about seventy five percent grey. I won't pretend that was an easy thing to come to terms with at first. But grey happened to be having a real moment in fashion, and I had multiple people stop me and ask what shade I'd used to get that beautiful grey. The answer was nothing. It was just mine. These days I don't colour my hair at all, and I save the entire cost every single time. In fact, my husband cuts my hair for me a couple of times a year.

One more small thing — use far less shampoo than you think you need. A blob roughly the size of a dollar coin is genuinely enough for most hair. Used this sparingly, a single bottle of shampoo lasts for months, sometimes way longer than that.

Nails

Keep nails short, trimmed and natural. It costs nothing, it's low maintenance, and it avoids the ongoing cost of regular manicures or gel fills. If you enjoy having some colour on your nails, a bottle of nail varnish applied at home costs a fraction of a salon visit and one bottle will last through dozens of applications.

Makeup and Skincare

Makeup is an area where most people are sitting on far more product than they realise, often unused for years out of habit rather than need. Use what you already have before buying anything new. I'm still working through eyeshadow palettes from my twenties — the only product I've found that genuinely goes off over time is mascara, which should be replaced regularly for hygiene reasons regardless. Everything else tends to last far longer than the packaging or the beauty industry would have you believe.

For everyday wear, a lip exfoliator followed by a lip balm or clear gloss does the job without needing a drawer full of different lipsticks and glosses in every shade.

The same "use what you have" principle applies to skincare and moisturiser. The last time I ran out of moisturiser, money was a little tight, so rather than buying a replacement straight away I worked through what else I had in the cupboard. First a leftover body butter. Then some leftover stretch mark cream — the cream version, not the oil, which I'd genuinely recommend avoiding on your face, the oil application didn't end well for me. And eventually, when I'd run out of everything else, a hand and nail cream. Months later, once money wasn't quite so tight, I finally bought the twenty dollar moisturiser I'd been wanting all along. In the meantime, my face survived just fine on whatever was already in the cupboard.

7

Keeping the Kids Happy and Entertained

Keeping kids entertained doesn't have to mean spending money, and in our house it rarely does. The instinct when kids are bored or restless is often to go somewhere — an indoor playground, a trampoline park, the cinema — but these come with entrance fees, the obligatory café snack because your own lunchbox isn't allowed in, and a bill that can easily run into hundreds of dollars for an afternoon. There is almost always a free or near free alternative that's just as fun, if not more so.

Free Days Out

The playground, the beach, your local domain, a river, a bush walk — all completely free, and all genuinely fun for kids when you make a proper occasion of it. Pack snacks, a drink bottle, or go further and take a full picnic. Many bigger parks have free BBQ facilities — make use of them and turn a simple outing into a proper family lunch out, without the restaurant bill. A cardboard box for 'sledging' on a grassy hill or sand dune is every bit as entertaining as a trampoline park, and costs nothing at all.

Movie Nights at Home

Instead of the cinema, with its inflated ticket and snack prices, bring movie night home. We have one on the first Friday of every month — a movie that's just been released to streaming or TV, a packet of popcorn, and whatever chocolate treat happens to be on offer that week. Because movie night comes around like clockwork every month, you can almost guarantee that at least one of your grocery shops that month will have popcorn and your go-to treats on special — ours is M&Ms — so plan around it and pick them up when the price is right.

Game Night

Saturday night was game night in our household for a while — board or card games we already own, no new purchases required. It costs nothing, the whole family can join in regardless of age — or at least that's the theory. Ours ran beautifully for years until the teenagers outgrew it and the little ones weren't quite old enough to properly join in. We're in the gap right now, but the games are stacked in the cupboard waiting, and I have no doubt game night will make a comeback when the youngest two catch up.

Homemade Fun

Building forts at home, whether from cushions and blankets indoors or branches and sticks outdoors, keeps kids occupied for hours at zero cost. Water play doesn't need a fancy play table

— a bucket of water, a paintbrush and an instruction to go and paint the fence will entertain most kids for a remarkably long time. A wash tub, some water and a handful of plastic animals turns into an hour of "cleaning" or an entirely invented muddy swamp adventure. A patch of dirt and some water can keep younger kids busy for an entire afternoon.

Homemade playdough is cheap to make and, stored properly in an airtight container, keeps for ages. Freezer toys are another favourite — freeze small toys into a block of ice and let the kids work out how to free them. Simple, cheap, and endlessly entertaining.

Sometimes the simplest option is the best one. Lying in the garden looking at clouds or searching under rocks for bugs costs nothing and kids genuinely love it.

Beyond that there's chalk for the driveway, a scavenger hunt around the garden, and stargazing on a clear night with nothing more than a blanket and maybe a stargazing app on your phone. Your local library is also worth checking regularly — most run free children's programmes, school holiday activities and reading challenges that cost nothing to join.

We're lucky in New Zealand that throughout the summer months there are often free events for children in most communities - a Christmas gala or a pop-up bouncy castle and sausage sizzle.

Toys, Birthdays and Christmas

In our house, toys are reserved for birthdays and Christmas. Not school holidays, not random Tuesdays, not because they were good at the supermarket. Two opportunities a year is genuinely enough, and it has real benefits beyond just the money saved.

It gives kids time to actually think about what they want, rather than impulsively requesting whatever they've just seen advertised. It gives you, as the parent, time to properly observe what your child actually plays with and gravitates towards, rather than guessing. And critically, it gives you time to source things second hand and to save up for them properly rather than scrambling for cash at the last minute.

I bought a bike for my daughter back in March, months ahead of her fourth birthday which isn't until August, after she'd mentioned wanting one. I found it on a local buy and sell page for $30. I bought it well in advance, specifically because I knew I had the money available right then, rather than waiting until closer to her birthday when the budget might have been tighter. Planning ahead like that, rather than shopping under pressure close to the date, is one of the simplest ways to make birthdays and Christmas far more affordable.

Buying for Christmas All Year Round

Christmas is the one date in the calendar you can always see coming, which makes it the easiest occasion to plan for well in advance rather than facing the full cost all at once in December.

We have a Christmas Eve box for each child every year, and it's always the same format — pyjamas, a mug, hot chocolate sachets, a chocolate Santa, and a book. Because the format never changes, I can buy each component whenever I happen to spot a good deal across the entire year, rather than scrambling to find everything in the same week in December.

Books get picked up from op shops or sales throughout the year, whenever something suitable for that child's age and interests turns up. Mugs are the same — whenever I see one that feels right for a particular child, it goes into the Christmas stash, regardless of what month it is. Christmas specific pyjamas can be bought for a fraction of the price in the days just after Christmas, once the entire range gets reduced to clear — buy a size up for the following year and they're ready and waiting twelve months later. Chocolate Santas and similar Christmas confectionery often go on sale at fifty percent off, or buy one get one free, in the weeks leading up to Christmas itself, so that's the one piece I tend to leave until closer to the date.

Actual Christmas presents follow a similar template based system — something to read, something to wear, something they want, something they need, and something to share. The categories stay exactly the same every year, which makes planning and budgeting far simpler, but what fills each category changes completely depending on the child and what they're into that year. It also naturally stops Christmas from spiralling into an enormous pile of expensive, impulse bought gifts, because the structure itself keeps things contained.

Subscriptions

There are a huge number of streaming services available now, but realistically one is sufficient for most families. Think about how your family actually consumes entertainment and choose the one that fits best — ours is currently Netflix, though that's not a fixed rule, just what works for us right now.

It's also worth knowing that most streaming services offer free trials, and there's nothing stopping you from cycling through them throughout the year. Use the free trial, cancel before it charges you, move to the next one when you want a change of content. Done well, you can go subscription free for considerably longer stretches of the year than most people realise, without ever feeling like you're missing out on anything.

None of this is about saying no to your kids or making them feel like they're missing out. If anything, it's the opposite. Some of our favourite family memories haven't cost us a cent — building a fort that took over the entire living room, an afternoon spent muddying every plastic animal we own in a washing tub, the same handful of board games played so many times the kids could probably referee them better than I can. Keeping kids happy has never really been about how much you spend on them. It's about the time, the attention, and the imagination you bring to what you already have.

8

Keeping the Kids Educated

Education is not a cost most families think of as optional or negotiable, but the cost of getting kids through it varies enormously depending on the choices you make and the school your child attends. This chapter looks at where the money typically goes, and the genuine options available to reduce it.

The Real Cost of Physical School

Even with free or low cost state education, the costs around school add up quickly. A school bag, a book bag, uniform, stationery, a lunch box, a drink bottle, and a laptop or device the school requires — that's before you've covered a single trip, camp, or the endless stream of fundraisers schools seem to expect contributions towards, from book club orders to cheese roll fundraisers.

Costs vary dramatically between schools, and I learned that the hard way. When my fourteen year old left correspondence school to attend a physical school, I was genuinely shocked to discover we needed around $600 just for school uniform and a laptop that met the school's specifications. It wasn't a cost I'd budgeted for, because our previous experience with school costs at primary school years earlier had looked nothing like that and our daughter's desire to return to face-to-face education kind of came out of the blue.

Reducing the Cost of Equipment

The bag, book bag, lunch box and drink bottle are all things that fit neatly into the "something they need" category of your Christmas gifting template, which we covered in the previous chapter. A new lunch box or drink bottle can just as easily replace a mug in a Christmas Eve box, or be slipped into a stocking, rather than being bought separately when the school year starts.

Uniform

Second hand uniform is widely available, either informally through community buy and sell groups or, in many schools, through an official second hand uniform shop run by the school itself. It's always worth asking if you're not sure whether one exists. Keep smaller sizes in storage as your children outgrow them if you have younger siblings coming through behind them — there's no reason to buy the same uniform item twice across multiple children.

It's also worth knowing that many schools have funding available specifically to help with uniform costs for families who need it. Sometimes all it takes is asking the school office directly. The same goes for school trips and camps — funding and discretionary support is often available for families who are struggling to cover the cost, but it usually isn't advertised loudly and there are certain criteria to be met. If a trip or camp cost is a genuine stretch, ask the school what support exists before assuming there's none.

Stationery

Every year a new stationery list arrives, and every year it can feel like you're expected to buy everything on it fresh. You're often not. A ruler, a calculator, highlighter pens and plenty of other items from the previous year are very likely still perfectly usable. Check what your child already has before buying anything new.

It also pays to shop around rather than automatically buying the bundled stationery pack offered by the school or its designated supplier. These bundles are convenient but often carry a premium, and the same items can usually be found cheaper elsewhere if you're willing to source them individually.

That said, factor your own time into that decision. Spending half an hour in a stationery store hunting for one specific type of paintbrush among a hundred similar looking options has a cost too, even if it's not a financial one. Sometimes paying the extra ten dollars for the convenience of the bundled pack is the more sensible trade off for your time and sanity. There's no single right answer here — just know that the choice exists.

Homeschooling and Correspondence School

It's worth stepping back and asking whether the traditional "go to school" model is actually the only option, or simply the default one most families fall into without considering alternatives.

Homeschooling removes most of the costs covered above

entirely — no uniform, no school bag, none of the fundraisers or bundled stationery packs — and families who are approved to home educate also receive an allowance to support the cost of their child's education.

Correspondence school, known in New Zealand as Te Kura, works similarly in terms of cost. Many of the physical school costs disappear, and the parent or caregiver supervising the child's learning receives a supervisor's allowance, along with additional support towards internet costs and, for those living rurally, financial support that recognises the particular circumstances of remote or rural learning. You can even get a loan laptop from Te Kura for the duration of your schooling.

Neither of these paths suits every family or every child, and there are obviously genuine considerations beyond just the financial ones — social connection, the support structures a physical school provides, and whether the model suits how your particular child learns best. But it's worth knowing these options exist and what they involve, rather than assuming a physical school is the only realistic choice. Education doesn't have to follow one fixed format. Think honestly about what works for your children, your family, and your finances, and don't be afraid to choose differently to what's expected.

Free and Low Cost Courses

Beyond school age education, there are often free or heavily subsidised courses and learning opportunities available if you go looking for them. My son did a barista course through our local polytechnic at no cost when he was 15 years old, and received free diving lessons through the local council's Mayor's Task Force for Jobs a Ministry of Social Development funded programme.

Opportunities like these tend not to be widely advertised, so if there's a skill you or your child wants to learn, it's worth asking around locally and searching online before assuming you'll have to pay full price for it. Polytechnics, local councils, rural support organisations like REAP and community groups all run programmes like this from time to time, and many of them cost nothing at all to take part in.

9

Keeping the Family Healthy

This is a shorter chapter than the others, and deliberately so. I'm not a health professional, and this isn't a chapter on nutrition or medical advice — there are far better qualified people to turn to for that. What I can offer is what we've actually learned and used ourselves around keeping medical costs down and keeping the kids active without spending much, if anything, at all.

Medical Care

In New Zealand, doctor's visits are free for children under 13. So if you have any concerns about your child's health, there's really no excuse for not making an appointment. For medical visits outside normal hours, because let's face it, kids don't pick convenient times to become ill, there is never a charge at Accident and Emergency. However it's worth noting that a lot of after-hours clinics do charge. Our first point of call after hours is always tele health. You can call the number, explain the issue and they will tell you the best course of action...that might be waiting until you can get into your GP or they might send you straight to A&E. If they are sending you to A&E, ask them to document why as it's often helpful during triage if the staff know that another medical professional has sent you.

For the rest of the family, a Community Services Card can significantly reduce the cost of GP visits and other services like ultrasounds, depending on the practice. The reduction varies from clinic to clinic, so it's worth checking your eligibility and, if you qualify, finding out which practices in your area offer the best rate for cardholders. Just like everything else in this book, it pays to shop around — not all GP practices charge the same amount, even for the same type of visit.

It's also worth being mindful about when a GP visit is genuinely necessary versus when it isn't. Not every minor cough, graze or worry needs an appointment, and learning to recognise what can be safely managed at home versus what needs a professional opinion saves both money and time. When in doubt, your local pharmacist is often a free first point of call for minor concerns, and Healthline is available for free advice over the phone if you're unsure whether something needs a doctor.

Keeping the Kids Active

Keeping kids active doesn't require an expensive gym membership or a packed calendar of paid activities.

If you have a Community Services Card, check whether your local swimming pool offers reduced entry or even swimming lessons for cardholders — many do, particularly in larger towns. In smaller rural communities, it's often the local school pool that's open to the public over summer, usually on a koha or donation basis, or for a small fixed fee that buys a key for the season. It's worth asking at your local school directly, as these arrangements aren't always advertised widely. Where it's safe to do so, rivers and, if you're in a warmer part of the country, the sea offer free swimming with no entry fee at all.

Many newer parks now come fitted with free outdoor exercise equipment alongside the usual playground gear — genuinely no gym membership required. A run around at the local playground is more than enough exercise for younger kids, and it costs nothing.

Make use of what you already have or can get cheaply. A trampoline is a significant outlay if bought new at full price, but they're regularly discounted in the lead up to summer and Christmas, so keep an eye out for a sale if it's something you're considering. People often off-load used trampolines when moving house too so you can often pick one up at a bargain price. They're a genuinely good investment for active outdoor play.

Bikes, scooters and skateboards turn up regularly and cheaply on local buy and sell pages, often free or for a token amount. It's also worth checking your local dump or transfer station — many have a group that restores bikes dropped off as rubbish and makes them available again, sometimes for free or a small donation. The same often applies to scooters and other ride-on toys.

Sometimes the simplest option is the right one. Just go for a walk — around the neighbourhood, to the local domain, or along a bush track. An obstacle course built from whatever you have lying around the garden — cushions, chairs, a hose to jump over, a washing line to duck under — can keep kids entertained and active for a genuinely long time.

On a wet day with no budget at all, YouTube has endless free kids' exercise and dance videos that turn an indoor, housebound afternoon into something active rather than another few hours in front of a screen doing nothing.

10

Keeping Afloat

Let's be honest about something most frugal living books tend to gloss over — not everyone reading this is working towards a comfortable surplus at the end of the month. Some of us are simply trying to get from one payday to the next without anything falling through the cracks. That's where we've been, more often than I'd like to admit, and if that's where you are too, this chapter is for you.

Living paycheck to paycheck doesn't mean you're failing at money. It means your income and your costs are closely matched, and managing that well is its own particular skill — different from saving, different from investing, and honestly, in some ways, harder than both.

Little Pots of Money

One of the things that's made the biggest difference for us is breaking the budget down into small, specific pots rather than treating it as one big number. On payday, a set amount goes straight into an account earmarked for rates. Another set amount goes into a pot for electricity. The money is allocated before it has the chance to disappear into general spending. For us this means when the monthly electricity bill lands, the money should already be in a pot waiting to pay it - no stress, no scrabbling, just quietly sitting there. Electricity is one of those expenses that is variable so we have to estimate what our bills are likely to be and set that aside. As ours fluctuates wildly from summer to winter we've found it easiest to pop the same amount in every payday, in summer the surplus sits in the account accumulating until the bigger winter bills arrive. If you've planned correctly, there will always be enough in the account - if you've over estimated it stays there until required, if you've underestimated, at least the bulk amount is there and it makes scrabbling for the extra a little easier than struggling to find the full amount.

A similar philosophy goes for our rates - ours are paid quarterly so are significant amounts each time. Again, it can be hard to find that large amount in one payday so transferring money into the rates pot every payday means the money is there when the bill lands. If you're able to switch to annual payments, you'll actually pay a little less because the council charges you a premium for the ability to pay in installments. This has always been my goal and for a couple of years we could do it but between the growing family, rising rates and house moves its currently not possible for us.

The Whiteboard

Alongside the pots of money earmarked for bills, we keep a whiteboard for everything else that comes up during the week — the things that aren't quite bills, but aren't quite nothing either.

Son needs new shoes. Mum wants quilting fabric. Christmas is coming and we need a new Christmas tree. We're fifty dollars short on the electric bill from last week. Whatever it is, it goes on the board as it comes up, rather than being bought or dismissed in the moment.

Then payday comes, and we go through the list together and actually talk about it. Mum's quilting fabric is a want, not a need, so it rarely makes it to the top of the list — though that doesn't mean it never gets there, it just means it sometimes has to wait its turn. Son hasn't got any extra activities on this week that specifically need trainers, so he can wear his walking boots instead, and that fifty dollars goes towards the electric bill we couldn't quite cover the week before.

The whiteboard does two jobs at once. It makes sure nothing important gets forgotten in the busyness of everyday life, and it stops impulse purchases dead in their tracks. Something goes on the board, sits there for a week or two or sometimes way longer, and more often than you'd expect it quietly comes off again — crossed out, never bought, because by the time payday came round it simply wasn't needed after all, or you'd found another way to accomplish the same goal.

It's not a glamorous system. It's a whiteboard in the dining room with a few scribbled words on it and sometimes, if we're super organised a price and a store name. But it's honest, it's visual, and it means every single dollar gets a conversation before it gets spent, which is about as much control as you can have when there genuinely isn't very much to go around.

Prioritise Needs Over Goals

When money is genuinely tight, the usual advice to "save first, spend second" doesn't always hold up. Sometimes the realistic priority order is transport to get to work, housing, utilities and food — in that order — and anything beyond that waits. There's no shame in that. Trying to force a savings habit on top of a budget that doesn't comfortably cover the basics often just creates more stress, not less. Cover the essentials first and let everything else come after.

Align Bills With Payday

Where you have any control over due dates, ask providers to move your bill dates closer to your payday. Most utility companies, insurers and even some loan providers will shift a due date if you ask. Less time between the money landing and the bill leaving means less opportunity for that money to get absorbed elsewhere before it's needed.

A Tiny Buffer, Even Five Dollars

A full emergency fund can feel like a complete fantasy when you're living week to week, but even a small, almost token amount tucked away regularly builds a buffer over time. It doesn't need to be a meaningful sum to start — even five or ten dollars a payday adds up, and having anything set aside reduces the chance of a small surprise expense turning into a real crisis or high interest debt.But here's the key point - if you can't pay for essentials, don't try to save. All you'll do is keep 'borrowing' the money and you'll be disheartened by the process with nothing to show for it at the end.

Don't Let New Debt Creep In

When things are tight, a credit card or buy-now-pay-later option can feel like the only way to cover a gap. Used occasionally and paid off quickly, that's manageable. Used regularly to bridge an ongoing shortfall, it usually makes the underlying problem worse, not better, because next payday now has to cover both the new bill and the one you deferred. If you're relying on credit to get through most weeks, that's worth being honest with yourself about sooner rather than later.

Unfortunately following my accident, we had to live off ACC payments for a while and as you may know, those are 20% less than your income. Mine was compounded by the fact that they took my 'income' from a Covid year so it didn't really reflect the true income I would have got. But that aside, we regularly popped a top-up food shop on the credit card, meaning to pay it off the following week. It was a small amount, smaller than the actual grocery shop but these few items week in week out, soon escalated and suddenly I had a hefty balance on my credit card - minimum payments felt like a blow and started meaning that we were running at a loss, every single pay day. So my advice, do not buy anything unless you have the available money to do so. Borrowing is not a convenient opportunity, it is a financial death sentence.

Small, Flexible Income on the Side

If you have any capacity at all, even an hour or two a week, a small amount of extra income can take real pressure off. It doesn't need to be a second job — babysitting, mowing a neighbour's lawn, selling something you've made, selling something you no longer need, doing a few hours of cleaning, documenting your life on YouTube, filling in online surveys. No amount is too small to matter when you're working with very little room to move.

When the Paycheck Genuinely Isn't Enough

Sometimes, no matter how carefully you've split it into pots, written it on the whiteboard and gone without, the paycheck simply doesn't stretch far enough to cover everything. That happens. It doesn't mean you've failed at any of this — it means your circumstances have outpaced what budgeting alone can fix, and that's the moment to look outward rather than trying to white-knuckle it through alone.

Ask your bank about a payment holiday on your mortgage or loan if you have one — most lenders have some provision for genuine hardship and would rather work with you than have you default on your payment. Call your power company and ask about a payment plan if a bill has gotten away from you. Stop by a food bank, as we talked about earlier in this book, without guilt or hesitation. Ask the school directly about support for uniform or trip costs if those are looming. Most of these forms of help exist quietly, waiting to be asked for, rather than being offered upfront — so the asking has to come from you.

There is no failure in needing help sometimes. The failure

would be staying silent about it and letting things spiral simply because asking felt harder than struggling alone.

11

Keeping Yourself Sane

This chapter is about you. Not the grocery budget, not the kids, not the mortgage — you, and the time and headspace you need to actually cope with everything else in this book. Financial worry can be completely consuming. It creeps into everything, sits with you at 3am, and makes it very easy to lose perspective. This chapter is about finding that perspective again.

Stop Comparing

It's worth saying plainly — comparison will quietly wreck your sense of perspective faster than almost anything else. Everyone shares their highlights on social media and very few people share their struggles. That new car was very possibly bought on finance. That exotic holiday might be the one indulgence in an otherwise tight year. Those fancy new clothes might be sitting on a credit card balance nobody else can see. You are looking at a carefully curated highlight reel and comparing it to your own full, complicated reality, and that's never a fair comparison to make.

Try to remember that you are living the best version of the life that's actually available to you right now, with the resources, circumstances and choices in front of you. That's worth more than measuring yourself against someone else's filtered version of theirs.

Find Something That's Yours

A hobby — something that's just for you, not for the kids, not for the household, not for anyone else — matters more than it might seem like it should when money is tight.

Some hobbies cost nothing at all. Walking, jogging, cycling. I'll be honest, I hate jogging, but plenty of people find it genuinely restorative. Reading, writing, drawing — all free, all just need a library card or a pen and paper.

But your hobby doesn't have to be free to be worth it, even on a tight budget. Mine genuinely isn't. I make quilts. I'm not an expert — still very much an amateur, learning as I go — but after our surprise baby arrived in 2022 I decided I wanted to make her a quilt for her first birthday. I learned to quilt from YouTube videos, my husband bought me an entry level sewing machine for my birthday, I bought some quilting fabric, and I just started. I've since made quilts for the rest of the family too.

The biggest ongoing cost is always the fabric, but I've found ways to keep that down — fabric off-cuts picked up cheaply at op shops, old bed sheets repurposed, all sorts of unlikely sources. On the tougher weeks, I simply use whatever I already have or I just don't quilt on these weeks. When I know my next quilt is coming up, I keep an eye out for VIP sales at places like Spotlight, and I pick up fabric secondhand throughout the year whenever I spot something useful. It's not a free hobby, but it's one I've made as affordable as I need it to be, and that flexibility is what makes it sustainable.

Knitting, crochet, embroidery, dressmaking, diamond art — these are all hobbies that can genuinely be as cheap or as expensive as you choose to make them. Start small, use what you can find secondhand, and let the hobby grow with your budget rather than waiting until you can afford to do it "properly."

A few more ideas worth considering if you're looking for somewhere to start: gardening, birdwatching, baking, puzzles, geocaching, learning a language through a free app, chess, journaling, photography on your phone, stargazing, or simply learning an instrument you already own or can borrow.

A Change of Scenery

Sometimes what you need isn't a hobby at all, just something different from your usual routine. A change of scenery, even a small one, can shift your headspace more than you'd expect. It doesn't need to cost anything — a different walking route, a different park, sitting somewhere other than your usual spot at home.

Free Courses

Keep an eye out for free online courses too, particularly if you find yourself with a bit of unexpected time on your hands. During Covid, with far more time at home than usual, I did both a crystal healing course and an angel healing course — purely because they were free, I was curious, and I had the time. Neither of those things became a career or a serious pursuit, but they kept my mind engaged during a genuinely strange and difficult period, and that mattered.

At Home Date Nights

If a proper date night is out of budget, it doesn't mean connection has to wait. An at-home date night can be just as meaningful — a different meal from your usual rotation, eaten after the kids are in bed, or sent to their rooms for the evening if they're old enough. The point isn't the venue or the cost, it's the deliberate time set aside for each other.

Grounding Yourself Outdoors

Find a small ritual that gets you outside, even briefly. For me it's as simple as making a homemade instant coffee and sitting with it in the morning, watching whatever's going on in the garden, before the rest of the day takes over. A few quiet minutes, no money involved, just space to actually be still.

Happiness Isn't About Consumption

If there's one thing worth carrying through this whole chapter, or in fact this whole book, it's this — happiness was never really about what you can buy. Find joy wherever you genuinely can, in ways big or small, and let that be enough. It usually is.

12

Keeping Going

You made it to the end of the book. That matters — not because finishing a book is a great achievement, but because the fact that you're here, reading this, means you're trying. You're thinking about your money, your family, your life, and how to make it all work with what you actually have rather than what you wish you had. That's not nothing. That's everything.

Financial Seasons

One of the things I wish someone had told me in my twenties, when I was earning well and spending freely and thoroughly enjoying both, is that financial life comes in seasons. There will be abundant seasons — periods where money flows relatively easily, where the bills get paid without drama and there's a little left over for something nice. And there will be lean seasons — periods where the whiteboard is full, the grocery budget has been squeezed to its absolute limits, and you're genuinely not sure how the next bill is going to get paid.

In my twenties I was firmly in an abundant season and I

assumed, without really thinking about it, that this was just how life would be. I spent it freely. I didn't save much. I certainly didn't plan for the possibility that things might look very different one day. I was young, I was earning, and I was absolutely not going to be one of those people who struggled to put food on the table or had to ask for help.

But I have been one of those people. More than once.

We've lived rent and mortgage free in a garage on the West Coast with no bathroom and wild weather battering the walls. We've had to take a loan out against the house, not to buy a home but to clear credit card debt that had quietly spiralled out of control. We've had abundant periods where life felt genuinely easy, and we've had periods where feeding the family was a real and daily concern. I've sat in a food bank and cried. I've budgeted thirty dollars to last a week. I've also sat at a table with good food, good wine and not a financial worry in the world.

None of those seasons lasted forever. That's the point.

If you're in a lean season right now, that's not your permanent address. It's where you are, not who you are, and it will change. The skills and habits in this book are what carry you through the lean times with as much dignity, warmth and full-stomached satisfaction as you can manage — and what quietly builds your resilience for the abundant ones.

Where We Are Now

We're credit card free. My husband is in a stable job, as stable as anything can really be in 2026 and the current economy. I'm a stay at home mum again after having our fourth child, or am I an author now? Let's wait and see. We're carrying a small ten year home loan but we're currently trying to sell a property after relocating, and in the meantime we're renting.

That might not sound like progress to some people. But for us, right now, it genuinely is. No annual rates bill increasing by ten or twenty percent every year. No home insurance on a very old house that costs a fortune and covers less than you'd think. No emergency fund required to fix a leaking roof or a failing water tank or any of the other unexpected costs that come with owning an older home. Just a fixed rental amount every week and someone else responsible for making — and paying for — the repairs.

It's not the endgame. We know that our financial situation will change as our lives do. One day we won't be responsible for a family of six — there will just be my husband and me, wherever that might be. A different season, a different set of needs, a different version of enough.

You Are Not Alone

Whatever your version of this looks like — whether you're feeding a family on thirty dollars a week, carrying debt that feels insurmountable, or just trying to get to the end of the month without the anxiety that's been sitting on your chest — you are not alone in it. Most people are managing something. Most people are carrying more than their social media would have you believe. Most people are figuring it out as they go, just like you, just like us.

This book was never about having all the answers. It was about sharing what we've actually learned, in actual circumstances, across an actual life that has looked nothing like the one I planned in my twenties. Some of it will work for you. Some of it won't. Take what's useful, leave what isn't, and know that just showing up and trying — even on the hard weeks, especially on the hard weeks — is enough.

You're doing better than you think.

Now keep going.

www.ingramcontent.com/pod-product-compliance
Lightning Source LLC
LaVergne TN
LVHW021737071126
851857LV00040B/1494
* 9 7 8 0 4 7 3 7 9 4 3 8 5 *

WORLD WAR TWO CAUSE AND EFFECT

By

BILL BRADY